Scot... Mot... g Century

Robert Grieves

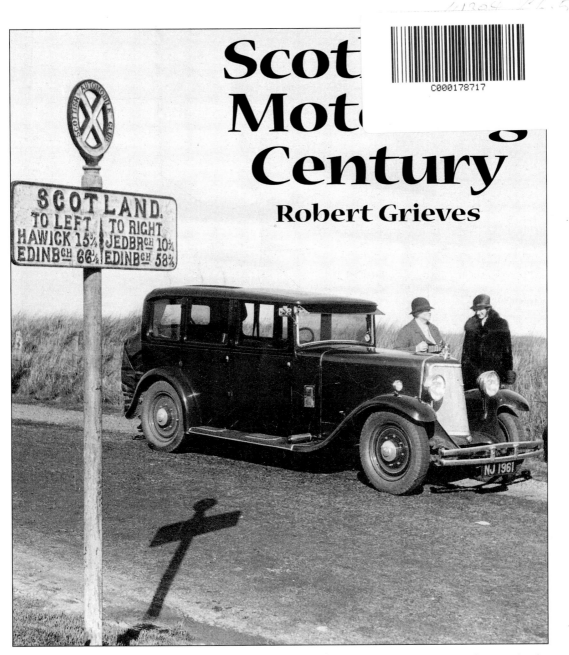

An Armstrong-Siddeley 20 hp saloon of 1933 complete with its famous Sphinx radiator mascot pauses before crossing the Cheviot Hills on the border at Carter Bar on what is now the A 68 road carrying one of the main routes southwards from Edinburgh to England via Jedburgh. The signpost showing distances in ¼ miles was erected by the Scottish Automobile Club (which celebrates its centenary in 1999) in Edwardian days when local councils seldom concerned themselves with such matters. The occupants of the car were probably holidaymakers heading home for the south of England as NJ 1961 was registered in East Sussex.

Front cover: A class-conscious sketch from 1907 showing the caddy tugging his forelock as a prosperous Edwardian family arrives at the golf links in their 16/20 hp Argyll tourer. Had the company survived, the Argyll car would have celebrated its centenary in 1999. First produced by Alex Govan at the Hozier Engineering Works in Bridgeton in 1899, a move was made in 1906 to the palatial new purpose built factory in Alexandria which survives today as Loch Lomond Factory Outlets which is a retail clothing warehouse.

Back cover: Motor manufacturing returned to Scotland in 1963 when the Rootes Group factory was opened in Linwood for the production of the Hillman Imp, their answer to the BMC Mini. This contemporary advert, courtesy of the former Rootes Group, features the 'Californian', a later member of the Imp range which was introduced in 1967, as was the 'Husky' estate car version. The final Imp rolled off the assembly line in March, 1976 but further cars such as the Hillman Hunter and Avenger and the Chrysler Sunbeam were manufactured at Linwood before the factory finally closed in May 1981.

Introduction

As the millennium year approaches it is natural that we should reflect on all areas of development. Being human we tend to think back in time as often as we contemplate the future. Because one of my special interests is motoring history I felt it appropriate to compile this album of photographs to illustrate the strides which have been made in this particular field. The motor car has been with us for little more than a century; indeed some of the oldest amongst us can recall when motor vehicles were still very much a novelty in the days when perhaps only the local doctor or the schoolmaster or the landed gentry in country districts had the means to afford an automobile. Today in contrast our traffic-clogged roads carry an incredible 29 million vehicles.

In that relatively short space of time the impact of the car has been such that there have been few inventions which have proved quite so important. Thanks to the motor vehicle wide areas have been opened up throughout the world to the ultimate benefit of everyone.

This photographic journey down memory lane, however, is confined to Scotland where most of my researches have been made. A few years ago I compiled a small volume entitled *Motoring Memories* which closed by saying 'Watch out for More Motoring Memories' which was to have been the sequel and despite the time lapse, *Scotland's Motoring Century* can now be regarded as that sequel and in a similar vein concentrates on the more historic earlier vehicles which today are no longer seen on our streets. Apart from the many motoring scenes in Scotland showing cars which started life in factories throughout Britain, Europe and America I have also included some of our own Scottish-built automobiles, few of whose manufacturers survived for long.

In many ways the history of the motor car slots neatly into the twentieth century. In the early 1900s the automobile was still in its infancy, although past the embryonic stage of the late 1890s when our first motor manufacturers appeared on the scene. Those pioneering years were bedevilled by restrictions not the least of which was an absurdly low speed limit of only 12 m.p.h. (raised to 20 in 1904) which begged to be broken, albeit at the risk of capture by a constable with a stop watch.

As this century closes, the wheels have turned full circle with the motorist once more having to suffer limitations and restrictions brought about by the car being very much a victim of its own success. The burdens of ever increasing road tax, fuel and insurance costs are compounded by traffic calming measures and attendant road closures in towns along with punitive parking penalties and the possible introduction of road tolls all aimed to discourage private transport. The car is no longer king and I suspect as the new century progresses, motorists may enjoy less freedom on the roads than ever before. The halcyon days of motoring are probably becoming a memory and so let's enjoy looking back as we turn these pages forward.

Greater emphasis has been given to the formative years of motoring. Early automobiles are acknowledged as veterans up to 1905 from which year the term Edwardian is valid beyond the death of the motoring monarch Edward VII in 1910 through until after the end of the Great War in 1918. The vintage period commenced in 1919 and continued through the reign of King George V until 1930.

Within these pages there is plenty of interest for motor devotees but I hope that a spark of enthusiasm may also perhaps be kindled amongst those who are unaware of Scotland's fascinating motoring past. I must make it clear, however, that this is not an attempt to be a definitive publication as inevitably I will be accused of having missed an item dear to someone's heart.

Enjoy the contents therefore which may help transport you back to the days long before so-called road rage was a familiar problem and when roads were certainly not the modern highways we have today but where motoring was a much more leisurely affair and accordingly a more enjoyable experience. Lest this seems too much of a sentimental viewpoint I must include a story from a contemporary motoring magazine of over 50 years ago which proves that nothing changes and we are really the same human beings as we always have been when we get behind the steering wheel. It also shows that the male v female supremacy thing as regards driving has been with us for more years than we might care to remember.

A small girl was taken to school by her father in the car each morning. One day father was ill and so mother drove her instead. That evening the little girl was speaking to her parent in his sickbed and said by way of conversation 'Oh, by the way, daddy we didn't meet any flaming idiots or bloody swine on the road this morning'.

Robert Grieves

First published 1999

ISBN 0 950638 14 5

© Robert Grieves

Typeset and printed by
Cordfall Ltd, Glasgow

Published by
XS Publications
66, Oakshaw Street
Paisley
PA1 2DE

Victorian Motoring

Before we progress in pictures through 20th century Scotland by car, let us briefly glance back to the final few years of the previous century when the birth of the automobile took place.

Scotland's first car was a Panhard et Levassor, built in Paris and imported from Antwerp to Leith in October 1895 for mainly experimental purposes by George Johnston of Glasgow. The honour of having been Scotland's first motorist, however, must go to Thomas Robert Barnewall Elliot of Clifton Park, Morebattle, Roxburghshire, a quiet village 6 miles from Kelso. He purchased a 3½ hp Panhard, similar to Johnston's and first drove it on the borders roads in December, 1895. This photo shows Elliot with his car outside Ednam House, Kelso which at that time was owned by the Duke of Roxburghe but is now a well established hotel. Elliot, who was to become 9th Laird of Harwood, was no doubt aware that his was the first automobile to be driven regularly in Scotland but was surely unaware that well within his own lifetime the motor vehicle would help shape the way of life for much of the world's population.

Last century there were extremely few who could claim 'motor driver' as a profession. One man who could was chauffeur Thomas Morrison of Edinburgh, seen here at the tiller of the first of a small fleet of Daimler dog-carts owned by pioneer automobile agents Rossleigh. The photo was taken in Edinburgh's Holyrood Park in 1897 when Morrison was 20. After service with the Royal Flying Corps during the Great War he started his own business as a garage proprietor and Austin agency in Dalry Road, Edinburgh.

3

The first motor manufacturer in Scotland was John Stirling of Hamilton who imported mainly Daimler and Panhard chassis from Europe which were then assembled with Daimler engines from Coventry and bodied in his Hamilton coachworks. He also operated a fleet of his own Stirling/Daimler wagonettes on what were Scotland's first primitive bus services in a variety of locations such as Hamilton, Falkirk, Ayr and Rothesay. This contemporary advertisement appeared in *The Automotor and Horseless Vehicle Journal* during 1897 and was almost certainly the first car advertisement featuring a Scottish product. Another 'first' for John Stirling was the opening of Scotland's original car showroom in Glasgow's Sauchiehall Street in 1899, where both Stirling's motor carriages and motor boats were on display.

The Stirling/Panhard dogcart was a popular light car around the turn of the century. This 5 hp model was a typical product of Stirling's factory in Hamilton, which transferred eastwards to Granton in 1902 to concentrate mainly on the building of commercial vehicles and buses. These purpose-built premises had previously been occupied by two short-lived automobile manufacturers. First was William Peck, the Edinburgh city astronomer, who constructed Madelvic electric carriages between 1898 and 1899 and which became Scotland's and perhaps Britain's first car company to collapse. Then followed the Kingsburgh Motor Construction Co. which lasted until Stirling's took over the factory in 1902. By 1906 no more vehicles were produced as Stirling had become another of the early casualties of the Scottish motor industry and the premises were then acquired by the Scottish Motor Engineering Co. Today part of these historic motor works still exists in Granton, now occupied by the United Wire Company where the original Madelvic logo of a chain-driven wheel may be seen above the office door.

The three 'A's; Albion, Argyll and Arrol-Johnston

Because of today's dearth of Scottish involvement with the motor industry, there are few of the present generation who would be aware that over the years Scotland has supported more than 50 different motor manufacturers! Most of these flourished then died in the first quarter of this century and perhaps the best-known were the three 'A's; Albion, Argyll and Arrol-Johnston, all of which were born towards the end of the 1890s and initially centred within a fairly close radius of each other in Glasgow. Both Albion and Argyll commenced business in 1899, in Finnieston and Bridgeton respectively, while the slightly older Mo-Car Syndicate which produced the Arrol-Johnston was based in Camlachie. Rapid expansion in those early days took all three to new locations. Albion moved to Scotstoun, Argyll to Alexandria and Arrol-Johnston to Underwood, Paisley and later to Heathhall, Dumfries.

Albion made the move from their cramped Glasgow premises in Finnieston Street to a spacious new purpose-built factory in South Street, Scotstoun in 1903. G 505 was an Albion A3 model built at the new factory in 1905 and was owned by J.D.W. Drysdale of Drysdale Pumps, Yoker. He is seen in the front passenger seat with his son at the wheel and other members of the family around the car while on a country drive from Glasgow. All are suitably dressed for the trip and wearing fashionable Edwardian motoring gear.

Contemporary advertising from 1905 features a 16 hp side (as opposed to rear) entrance tonneau on the popular model A3 chassis which enjoyed a long run of success. Somewhat surprisingly the advert extols the virtues of solid tyres, which were rapidly ousted by pneumatics as the Edwardian era progressed. Albion, however, always maintained a reputation for reliability often at the expense of modernity and admittedly early pneumatic tyres were often a source of trouble as regards frequent punctures. Even at this early stage it can be seen that Albion had built up a surprising number of agencies in Scotland. Although not listed here, the rest of Britain and colonial countries were also well represented by company agents.

A later Albion to be produced at the Scotstoun works was the A6 type. This was a larger 24/30 hp model which proved popular with families who were in a sufficiently comfortable financial position to afford the employment of a chauffeur. A typical example is seen here with the ladies in their elaborate Edwardian outfits primarily intended for motor journeys. The uniformed chauffeur stands at the front of the car which was of landaulette style featuring enclosed coachwork but with a rear compartment fitted with a hood which could be folded down on fine days. XS 197 was registered in Paisley in 1909 and was owned by A.F. Craig, a successful ironfounder in the town who may be seen beside the ladies.

A line of Glasgow taxi cabs built in 1909 on Albion A3 type chassis. This scene dates from December 1914 and was taken on the occasion of the visit of the Chinese Prince Zai Sunn and his entourage to the armour plate works at Wm. Beardmore's Parkhead Forge. The leading two cabs were registered G 1817/8. Although Albion's automobiles proved popular their commercials were even more so and in 1913 the company decided to cease production of private cars and concentrate on their range of heavy vehicles. Albion trucks and buses with their well-known traditional radiator and 'Sure as the Sunrise' badge achieved world-wide success for their solid reliability. Today owned by the American Axle & Manufacturing Co., of Detroit, Albion now produces only axles and components. Nevertheless it has been the only Scottish motor manufacturer to survive a century with the company celebrating its centenary in 1999.

Alexander Govan's Argyll motor car was produced by Hozier Engineering of Bridgeton from 1899 until 1905 when the company changed its name to Argyll Motors. This 1901 advert shows the 5 hp Argyll voiturette which was on public display that year at the Glasgow International Exhibition at Kelvingrove. As with Albion, 1999 would have marked the hundredth birthday of Argyll, had the company survived.

Under the expertise of Alex. Govan the Argyll went from strength to strength in a remarkably short space of time. The 4 cylinder 16 hp model as seen here was available in 1903 and this pneumatic tyred e xample was undertaking the then arduous journey down from Inverness to Edinburgh and tackling the Drumochter Pass between Dalwhinnie and Blair Atholl when photographed near Dalnaspidal. In those early days a contemporary road guide book described the surface of this main route as 'poor and overgrown with grass in some parts' which now seems incredible when compared with today's fast modern A9 highway. The first major reconstruction and surfacing work to be carried out on this road took place between 1925 and 1928 hampered by a General Strike and bad weather. The car pictured here was owned by pioneering motor engineers Rossleigh of Edinburgh and its driver was the same Thomas Morrison as seen on p. 3.

John Boyd Dunlop was born in Dreghorn, Ayrshire, in 1839 and was originally a veterinary surgeon prior to the renown achieved for the early development and resultant success of the pneumatic tyre (originally invented by Robert Thomson of Stonehaven) He owned several Argyll cars over the years and in this scene from 1902 we see Dunlop in a Bridgeton-built 10 hp model driven by his daughter with the chauffeur taking a back seat on this occasion. Naturally we must assume that it was shod with Dunlop pneumatics which undoubtedly made a huge contribution to the success of early motoring mainly due to the improvement in both comfort and speed which his invention made possible.

The advertisement reproduced below shows contemporary publicity for Dunlop tyres when the company exhibited at the 1913 Olympia motor show in London.

The elegant and handsome bodies of the Argyll
Cars are well in keeping with that perfection of
mechanism which has made the reputation of

The FAMOUS ARGYLL. 1906

Made only from the best selected materials, finished in the
highest class style, and upholstered in leather and best
quality horsehair, they present a perfect example of the
coach-builder's craft. ————————————————————

Over a dozen types of bodies are made, amongst which the most fastidious will have no
difficulty in making a satisfactory choice.

ARGYLL MOTORS, Ld., ALEXANDRIA, by GLASGOW.

London Agents: ARGYLLS, LONDON, LTD., 17, Newman Street, Oxford Street, W.

Argyll advertisement from 1906, just after their move from Bridgeton to Alexandria. The company publicity department
was always in the forefront of advertising in newspapers and motoring journals and usually produced entertaining copy.
   The police constable holds a stop watch and in collaboration with a colleague hidden along the road would be trapping
unwary drivers for speeding in excess of the 20 mph limit then in force.

Later in the decade, this scene from 1910 was posed outside the main entrance to the grand new purpose-built factory which the Argyll company occupied in Alexandria from 1906. What appears to be a car-cramming competition was actually the Argyll directors and their company chauffeur David Buddie taking part in a publicity photograph advertising the 'Flying Fifteen' which was the popular name for this new 15 hp model. Argyll's manager Colonel John Smart Matthew, standing in front of the car, is one of the fifteen people in this view.

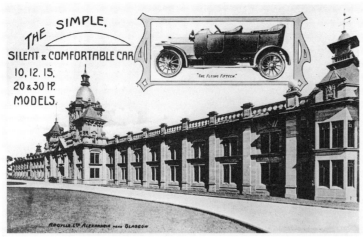

An advertising post card produced by Argyll showing their 'Flying Fifteen' inset above the palatial factory at Alexandria which proved to be a drain on resources and never used to full capacity. After several troubled years the company again went into liquidation in 1914 and ownership of the factory changed hands. The following year a new Argyll company under the leadership of John Brimlow opened in the former works at Bridgeton where fitful production took place until 1928. At least the fine Edwardian factory at Alexandria can still be enjoyed today as the restored building now houses Loch Lomond Factory Outlets, a retail clothing warehouse which includes a small transport museum.

A 12/18 hp Argyll with grey finished 'torpedo' style body built in the Alexandria coachbuilding department. This car was purchased in August 1913 by confectionery manufacturer William Archibald of Shand Street, Wishaw (who remembers Archibald's 'Battleaxe' toffee?) and is seen at the main entrance to Belhaven Estate, Glen Road, Wishaw. The registration number SB 533 was an Argyllshire issue but many owners from elsewhere deliberately licensed their cars in that county in order to appropriately obtain an Argyll index mark. Note the front wheel brakes which were a feature on Argyll cars long before other manufacturers even considered four wheel braking; and what a pair of headlamps!

The Mo-Car Syndicate was registered in December 1898 with much of the capital subscribed by civil engineer Sir William Arrol (flush from his success with the Forth Bridge). The name Arrol-Johnston, however, was given to their cars and that shown here was reputedly the first production model in the late 1890s, with founder George Johnston whose engineering skills caused it to happen, seated beside business partner Norman Fulton who has his left hand on the tiller steering. This was a 6-seater model which the company described as a car, whereas their 4-seater was known as a dog-cart and the rugged but antiquated design remained in production surprisingly until 1905. The location here was Johnston's home at Mosesfield House, Springburn, where in the coach house he had built and experimented with motor car engines in those days of the embryonic automobile.

Arrol-Johnston cars were initially built at Camlachie in the east end of Glasgow but after a disastrous fire in 1901 a move was made the following year to Underwood in Paisley where a former thread mill was provided by the Coats family who were also shareholders in the Mo-Car Syndicate. This 6 seat car was built at Paisley and differs little from the original model. A wheel as opposed to tiller steering is fitted and this view clearly shows the seating arrangement of two in front of the driver and two behind who could admire the disappearing scenery. The location here is John O' Groat's hotel in 1903, the young lady at the wheel having driven all the way from Land's End and is believed to have been the first female to have accomplished this. Miss Murison (contemporary reports shyly do not give her first name) was from Kilkenny in Ireland and was only 19 at the time which no doubt caused a degree of commotion in those staid veteran days, but provided perfect publicity for Arrol-Johnston.

Sir William Arrol withdrew from the Mo-Car Co. in 1905 and his position was filled by William Beardmore, another well-known Scottish industrialist, who immediately injected new life into the ailing business. Production of the antiquated dog carts ceased and a completely new and attractive design appeared to combat the many rivals on the scene, illustrated here by ST 153, described as a New Arrol Johnston. This was a 1908 example and was delivered when new to garage proprietor A.W. Chapman of Church Street, Inverness, later passing to David Fraser of Dunkeld Street, Aberfeldy.

A company invoice from 1906 which shows the deleted name of the Mo-Car Syndicate replaced by The New Arrol-Johnston Car Co.

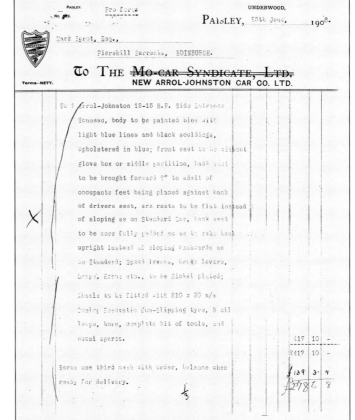

Vignette showing the clean lines of a 1911 Arrol Johnston 15.9 hp tourer as seen driven by Jackie Stewart (below)

In 1909 a new and experienced general manager came to oversee the Paisley works. He was Thomas Charles Pullinger who had previously been with Sunbeam and Humber and was the driving force behind the development of an Arrol Johnston 15.9 hp model featuring a Renault-style bonnet with the radiator placed behind, clearly shown in this illustration of LE 8582 a 1911 example which survives today in Glasgow's marvellous Museum of Transport. At the wheel with his wife Helen is a young Jackie Stewart, Formula 1 racing driver from 1965–73 and triple world champion who was more often pictured in somewhat speedier situations. The location here was Albert Drive, Glasgow, outside the original Museum of Transport.

Edwardian Miscellany

The Edwardian era was so important in the early development of the automobile that I make no apology for featuring more scenes which depict some of the multiplicity of makes marketed during a period of huge competition for the customer who must have been spoilt for choice but no doubt somewhat confused as well. Apart from a huge number of English and European chassis available the products of no less than 20 Scottish-based motor manufacturers were advertised in the mid-Edwardian period alone. Alphabetically these ranged from T. & R. Taig's Alexis built in Alexandria to the Werbell in Dundee (see p. 19), many of which were admittedly obscure to say the least, producing only a few vehicles and in some cases just a single car.

The world's first mass-produced car was Ransom Eli Olds' curved dash Oldsmobile from Lansing, Michigan, USA and popular as a town runabout. Many were imported to Britain and this example from 1903 found its way to Bridge of Allan, where it was owned by Colonel Edward Alexander of The Red House, Pendreich Road, who is seen here with his wife outside their home. The Colonel's left hand is resting on the tiller steering where the warning device of a bulb horn has been attached. This little car (painted black) was registered MS 2 in Stirlingshire when vehicle licensing commenced there in December 1903.

Also registered in Stirlingshire was MS 66, although its first owner lived in Fife. The car was a dark green Gladiator 12 hp tonneau imported from France and purchased in March 1904 by John Alistair Erskine Cuninghame of Balgownie House, Culross, the location of this family photo. Cuninghame was Provost in this historic Fife town for 42 years where his commemorative plaque may be seen today outside the Town House.

The well known Glasgow engineering firm G. & J. Weir of Cathcart built three racing cars in 1904 on behalf of the French Darracq company which was eager to win the prestigious Gordon Bennett Cup that year. In addition to Darracq's own French team and in order to have more than a sporting chance, three other replica Darracqs were to be built by Opel in Germany and three in Britain as in order to comply with the competition rules cars entered for the race had to be made wholly in the country they represented. William Weir was himself a keen motorist and a director of the Darracq concern, thus readily accepting the formidable challenge to construct the three British entrants in the short space of ten weeks. The job was completed in time and although these 90/100 hp Weir-Darracqs proved unsuccessful in the 1904 event they performed well subsequently. Interesting points regarding fitments on these racers were their steering column gear change and live axles as opposed to the gate change and chain drive which were generally more usual on cars of that period.

An Aster engined St Vincent car which was built in Glasgow by William McLean who had started constructing cycles in premises at the corner of St Vincent Street and North Street before progressing to motor vehicles around 1903. His later cars were often referred to as Scottish Asters. GG 4 was an early Glasgow-issue dealer's number or trade plate and was not a registration number until 1930.

Typical of the Kelvin cars described below was this 16 hp example from 1906 which took part in that year's Reliability Trial organised by the Scottish Automobile Club (now the Royal SAC) in which it fared commendably. G 874 is seen with Kelvin founder Walter Bergius at the wheel passing through the main street of Pitlochry where the entrants stayed at Fisher's Hotel on the third evening of the four day event. A good crowd including barefoot boys was there to spectate since it must be remembered that motor vehicles were still relative rarities and to see so many together was a special occasion. It is followed by ES 226, a Perthshire registered Renault which was not a trial entrant.

In May, 1904, the Bergius Car and Engine Co. commenced business in Finnieston Street Glasgow in Albion's original premises which had been vacated for expansion at Scotstoun. The founder and proprietor Walter Bergius had previously worked with Albion before deciding to produce motor cars on his own account and the first was built before the year's end and named the Kelvin. Not many more than a dozen Kelvin cars were constructed between 1904 and 1906 but much more success was enjoyed through production of the Kelvin Marine Engine, built by the Bergius company in their new factory in Dobbies Loan, Glasgow. Some of the Kelvin cars were bodied by pioneer Glasgow coachbuilders Alex. Cree & Co. of Kelvindale Street, who were described in contemporary directories as 'cabinetmakers and bodybuilders.' Cree also built Albion cars and is reputed to have bodied the first car constructed in Scotland which was George Johnston's prototype of around 1896 for the Arrol-Johnston which followed later.

Many of the early motor manufacturers in Scotland produced only a handful of vehicles before abandoning their plans, usually for financial reasons. It was virtually impossible to compete successfully with the big boys of the time such as the 3 'A's. One of the earliest of these small enterprises was owned by garage proprietor John Tavendale whose premises were at 74 High Street, Laurencekirk, in the fertile Mearns area of Kincardineshire. Around the turn of the century he produced a small number of cars which he appropriately named 'St Laurence' with Accles-Turrell 6 hp engines. Watched by the usual interested crowd of youthful spectators, a St Laurence of about 1901 is seen near its birthplace.

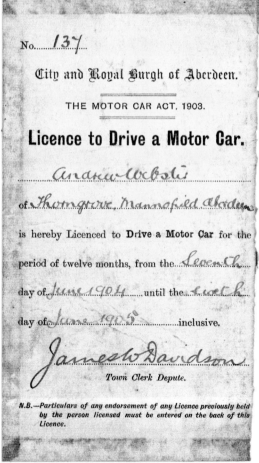

No. 137

City and Royal Burgh of Aberdeen.

THE MOTOR CAR ACT, 1903.

Licence to Drive a Motor Car.

Andrew Webster

of Thorngrove, Mannofield, Aberdeen,

is hereby Licenced to **Drive a Motor Car** for the period of twelve months, from the Seventh day of June 1904 until the Sixth day of June 1905 inclusive.

James W Davidson
Town Clerk Depute.

N.B.—Particulars of any endorsement of any Licence previously held by the person licensed must be entered on the back of this Licence.

As the number of the new-fangled automobiles increased, Parliament passed legislation such as the Motor Car Act of 1903 which included licensing both for vehicles and for their drivers. Registration index marks were introduced and local authorities were empowered to grant drivers licences. The very early example reproduced was issued in Aberdeen in 1904 to Andrew Webster of Thorngrove, Mannofield who was chauffeur to prominent engineer William Jackson who owned RS 1 (see p. 21). Although licences were thenceforth a legal necessity no form of driving test was required as it was assumed applicants were fully adept with the appropriate skills.

At the other end of Scotland in Newton Stewart, Wigtownshire, Messrs. Murchie and Picken who were later the local agents for both Austin and Ford built about a dozen motor cycles and at least one car, which is pictured here. Locally registered OS 3 in April, 1904, was a 10/12 hp Murchie car owned by Doctor William Selby of Port William.

Also in the south of Scotland, Drummond's Dumfries Brass and Iron Foundry of Pleasance, Dumfries (renamed the North British Motor Manufacturing Company in 1906) built about thirty North British or Drummond cars in that town between 1903 and 1910. Most found buyers around the county but some were 'exported' over the border to England and one as far as Rio de Janeiro in Brazil. This 1907 advert was unintentionally prophetic as within a year or two the sands of time had run out for the Drummond.

The Dalhousie car with its steeply raked radiator was certainly a sporty looking machine but was only built in very small numbers. The maker was George Anderson (1905) Ltd. of Carnoustie, Angus, who was perhaps better known later in the Anderson-Grice partnership for manufacturing foundry equipment. Seen here is SR 210 which was a 2 seat model registered in the name of its maker George Anderson in June 1907. The Dalhousie name must have been bestowed to this company's cars in later life, as original registration details for both this example and SR 249 which was a 4 seater of 1908 owned by Arthur Grice of Arbroath give no mention of it and show only '4 cylinder' in the maker's name column.

Also in the same county and around the same time, the brothers William and Edward Raikes-Bell in Dundee built the 25 hp White and Poppe engined Werbell car, one of which is seen outside their motor engineering premises in 1908. It is doubtful whether any more than a few Werbells were built over the period between 1907 and 1910 but nevertheless there was a distinguished customer for a 5 seater 25 hp model built in 1909 which was purchased by the Earl of Strathmore at Glamis Castle and registered SR 264. On cessation of car building William Raikes-Bell concentrated on operating his Forfarshire Motor Bus Co. based in South Ward Road Dundee with a small fleet of Halley charabancs. For a predominantly rural county Angus produced a surprising number of small scale motor makers since there was also the Fraser steam car in Arbroath and the Adamson which was a one-off 'own make' from Brechin, both in 1913.

Apart from the Arrol-Johnston company in Paisley during the reign of King Edward VII, there were two other very much smaller motor manufacturers in the textile town. James McGeoch of Incle Street produced light two seat 3-wheelers named the 'Seetstu' which was a play on words as Seestu is an old name for the town and John Ridley of George Place built the Ridley car which was also a two-seater (plus two rear facing) as seen here. He had previously built cars in Coventry but moved to Paisley around 1906.

MS 456 was registered in April 1910 to Donald MacLean of Peatriggend House, Slamannan, Stirlingshire and was a single cylinder 7 hp Ridley which was recorded as having interchangeable dog cart and van bodies. A similar Ridley took part in the 1906 Scottish Automobile Club reliability trial.

Ladies in the driving seat at the Lochinvar Hotel, Dalry, Kirkcudbrightshire. This mid-Edwardian scene shows an early Bridgeton-built two cylinder Argyll from about 1902 (registered G 214 in Glasgow when vehicle licensing started there in 1904) in company with a new four cylinder Daimler tourer. An island castle in Lochinvar was home to the 'Young Lochinvar' of the famous ballad.

A most impressive machine poses complete with uniformed chauffeur in front of its owner's equally impressive home. This was an imported 18 hp Panhard Levassor phaeton from Paris (terms used by builders of horse-drawn coaches were often still used by motor manufacturers to describe bodywork styles). It was finished in a dark red livery and fitted with acetylene headlamps and paraffin side and tail-lamps and a magnificent horn, all of which were brass and had to be kept gleaming by the chauffeur. The owner of all this was Christopher Haigh Morris of Baron's Craig, which overlooks the Solway Firth at Rockcliffe near Dalbeattie, Kirkcudbrightshire, who registered SW 54 in January 1907. Baron's Craig is now an attractive private hotel.

An interesting trio of Coventry-built cars in 1904 at Aberdeen. The little single cylinder Rover in the centre with the ladies was RS 161, flanked on each side by Maudslay 25 hp six cylinder landaulettes RS 1 and 144. The former was the first motor vehicle licensed in Aberdeen and was owned by local businessman William Jackson of 'Thorngrove', Mannofield, who had made his fortune developing tea processing machinery in Assam. He was also a director of the Aberdeen Tramway Company. Maudslays were perhaps better known for building commercial vehicles and the very first buses to be operated by the SMT Company in Edinburgh were of this make in 1906.

A magnificent Maudslay. A link existed between Aberdeenshire and the Maudslay Motor Co. because Sir Charles Forbes of Newe, Strathdon, was the company chairman and members of his family and their friends naturally patronised this make. The Great North of Scotland Railway Company, based in Kittybrewster, Aberdeen operated Maudslay buses as feeders to their railway services in the county prior to World War 1. In comparison to the early Maudslay cars seen in the previous view, SA 163 is an example of a 1910 model, new to the Farquharson family of Whitehouse by Alford and pictured here at Brux near Kildrummy. This was a 4 cylinder 17/20 hp model with the distinctive round radiator usually associated with Maudslay cars but also similar to that fitted to the French Delaunay-Belleville of the same period. This particular car is also noteworthy for its electric lamps and horn which were advanced fittings at that time.

Another popular make in veteran times was the Napier, built in London. Aberdeen registered RS 86 was a 1904 model and is seen in Union Street, the main thoroughfare through the Granite City while one of the Corporation tramcars passes bound for Rosemount. The occasion was the visit of an African Nabob, from Abeokuta (now in Nigeria) in July 1904 which attracted a fair bit of interest judging by the crowd.

Many of the Edwardian illustrations show the drivers and passengers in typical motoring clothing of the period, which in comparison with today's gear appears as if the wearers were over-dressed to say the least. But it must be remembered that the majority of cars were open to the elements—the wind, rain, hail and snow of winter and the often choking dust of the unmade roads in summer. Naturally therefore their garb had to reflect driving conditions. Outfitters stores such as Paisley's or Copland & Lye in Glasgow specialised in clothing for the increasing number of motorists, or automobilists as they were then known. George Paisley was himself a keen motoring enthusiast.

It is generally accepted that the Lanchester brothers from Birmingham produced the first car to be made in Britain (although George Johnston in Glasgow gave them a close run). Braking, gear-changing and steering on Lanchester cars were all controlled by levers, only the acceleration being pedal operated. This Dunbartonshire registered model was a 4 cylinder 28 hp landaulette owned around 1908 by Dumbarton shipbuilder Sir Archibald Denny. The photo was taken at Cardross Park which was the Denny family estate with chauffeurs William Adie (driving) and Jim Campbell.

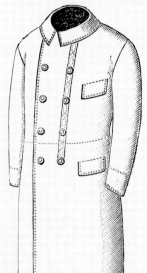

Children's pedal cars gained popularity in the Edwardian era in pace with the real thing on which they were based, although just like the real thing it was only the more affluent who could afford to purchase a toy car for their child. This very early chain driven model from the first years of this century was probably based on the popular Renault of the period and is seen with its proud occupants near Coldingham in Berwickshire.

'Just like uncle's!' Here we see Master Peter Keith Murray who was the lucky small owner of a pedal car around 1909. This car was built by G. & J. Lines (later Lines Bros. and from 1931 Tri-ang) who were the best known manufacturers of children's vehicles for many decades (I had one in the 1950s). Uncle was Sir William Keith Murray of Ochtertyre, Perthshire and his car was the elaborate 18 hp Wolseley Siddeley fitted with wire spoked wheels like its small relation.

24

An Edwardian photo selection would be incomplete without illustrating the Rolls-Royce which had the reputation of being 'The best car in the world'. R 534 was delivered to the Marquis of Bute in August 1908 and was an example of the 40/50 hp 'Silver Ghost' which had been introduced in 1907 and remained in production for a lengthy run of 19 years. This one was fitted with Barker coachwork of the 'Roi des Belges' style which described luxurious open touring bodywork and named after King Leopold of Belgium. We see the Rolls in the 1950s by which time it was owned by John C. Sword, general manager of the Western SMT bus company and an avid collector of veteran and vintage cars. The location is Craigweil, his former home on the seafront at Ayr which is now a youth hostel.

A 40/50 hp Rolls-Royce 'Silver Phantom' of 1909 with touring coachwork also by Barker and registered R 567 in Derby to where the factory had moved from the original Manchester premises. It is negotiating one of a series of severe hairpin bends on the isolated hill road which climbs through Glen Quaich between Amulree and Kenmore, Perthshire, where it zig-zags above Garrow Farm, with Loch Freuchie visible in the distance. This took place during a testing tour over Scottish roads which was driven personally by Claude Johnson who was then managing director of Rolls Royce Ltd.

Doctors, who were amongst the few folk financially able to enjoy the benefits of a motor car at the start of the century, tended to favour two-seaters. Certain manufacturers actually described their two seat models as 'doctors' cars'. This was a typical example which was owned around 1908 by Doctor Calder of Kirkhill, Coldingham, Berwickshire where the photo was taken. X 1076 was registered across the border in Northumberland and was a Coventry-built Swift. Seen in the car is John Johnstone, the doctor's chauffeur, who later set up his own business as a mechanic and engineer with backing from the doctor.

This was Montgomery Street in Eaglesham in 1912. Today it carries an unacceptable amount of heavy traffic through this attractive conservation village to and from the main Kilmarnock Road across Fenwick Moor. However, in those days traffic was sparse and this new Italian Alfa car must have been a real rarity, causing consternation to the local ducks, geese and horses. Alfa stood for Anonima Lombardo Fabbrica Automobili of Milan (the Lombardy Motor Manufacturing Co.) which was later to become Alfa Romeo.

To Owners of Cars.

LADIES AND GENTLEMEN.
Do You Understand all about Your Car?
IF NOT—WHY NOT!!

THE SCOTTISH SCHOOL OF MOTORING

Is the only School in Scotland devoted entirely to the Practical Teaching of Driving, Running Repairs, and Economy in the Up-keep of the Automobile.

DAY AND EVENING CLASSES—INCLUSIVE FEES.

Write, Call or 'Phone :—

Workshops and Garage—**22-30 SHAMROCK STREET, W.**

Offices and Institute—**3 ELMBANK CRESCENT (near King's Theatre), Glasgow.**

Telephones—Central 3111, Offices and School.   Douglas 345, Workshops and Garage.   W. MADDISON, General Manager.

Incredibly, many Edwardian owners were unable to drive their own cars and simply employed a chauffeur who was also trained in the mysteries which took place below the bonnet. Many early motor manufacturers provided a training course for chauffeurs which not only taught them how to drive the make in question but also how to maintain it. Subsequently if the car owner himself decided to learn then it was generally the chauffeur who imparted the knowledge. As the years progressed and the car became less of merely a plaything for the rich, motoring schools were founded to provide the necessary driving skills, typical of which was the Scottish School of Motoring in Glasgow. This scene from 1921 shows a 1913 Humber and a 1907 Renault which were two of the training cars outside the school headquarters in Elmbank Crescent.

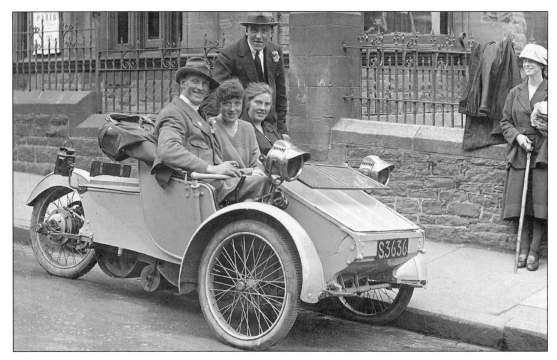

The Autocarrier was a popular little three wheeler with seats for two (or three if you squeezed up as in this instance). Known usually as the A.C. Sociable, it hailed from Thames Ditton in Surrey and featured a two speed epicyclic gearbox and tiller steering. S 3636 was registered in Edinburgh in 1913 and is seen in Penicuik.

SA 1317 was an Aberdeenshire registered Belsize tourer seen on a chauffeur driven outing when new in 1913. This Manchester based manufacturer also produced commercial vehicles and taxis but by 1925 was in the hands of the receiver.

In the early days of motoring, radiators were all shapes and sizes which must have been an enjoyable challenge to youthful car spotters of the time. Four examples are shown:

The radiator of the 10/12 hp Rover had the appearance of a shield. Renfrewshire registered HS 170 was a 1910 model first licensed to John Paton, Rosebank, Bishopton and later passing to Bertie Gibson, West Arthurlie Cottage, Barrhead, where it is seen about 1911 when it was one of very few cars in that locality.

Today the name Dennis is particularly associated with buses, fire engines and trucks, but here we see BS 103 a Dennis landaulette of 1911 which was owned by Robert Garden, a general merchant based in Kirkwall in the Orkney Islands. Dennis Bros. of Guildford discontinued car production from 1913 to concentrate on their more successful commercial vehicle range (as did Albion Motors).

A 15 hp Valveless touring car built in Huddersfield and as yet unregistered when the photo was taken at South Queensferry about 1912 but showing Edinburgh trade plates SF 9.

A German import from Stettin was the Stoewer which was relatively unknown in this country unless a local agent existed. Macrae & Dick of Inverness were agents for the north of Scotland and this 1912 model carries their trade plates while on a demonstration run.

A fondness for *Ford* ...

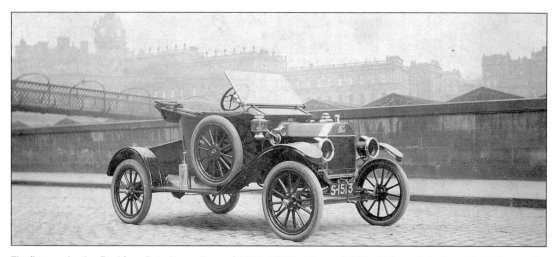

The first production Ford from Detroit was the model 'A' in 1903 but the model 'T' which was introduced in 1908 was to be the car which ensured immortality for Henry. The 'Tin Lizzie', which had only two forward speeds with pedal controlled transmission was produced for 18 years during which time over 15 million were built. This non-standard example of the rugged little car is S 1513, an Edinburgh registered two seater pictured prior to World War I in the city's Market Street looking over Waverley Station and the tower of the former North British Hotel towards Princes Street.

An event which gave a great deal of publicity to the then fledgling model 'T' and considerably boosted sales not only in Scotland but throughout Britain was the successful attempt to drive in one to the summit of Ben Nevis. This feat was made in 1911 by Henry Alexander whose father owned the main Ford agency in Edinburgh and S 1871, which was a 1910 model, is seen at the weather station and observatory which was then on the 4,406' mountain top. This had closed in 1904 but until the end of the Great War the small observatory hotel remained open, serving the highest teas in the country!

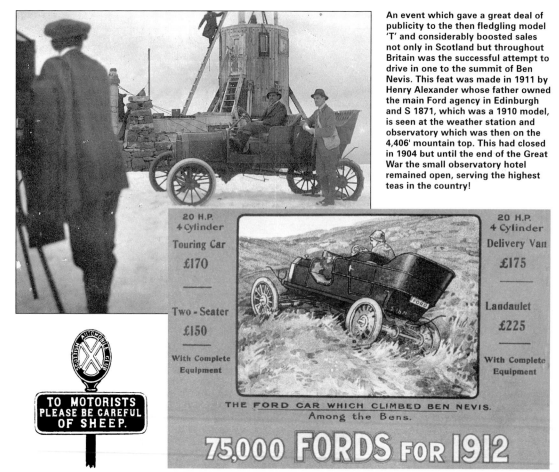

TO MOTORISTS PLEASE BE CAREFUL OF SHEEP.

20 H.P. 4 Cylinder		20 H.P. 4 Cylinder
Touring Car £170		Delivery Van £175
Two - Seater £150		Landaulet £225
With Complete Equipment		With Complete Equipment

THE FORD CAR WHICH CLIMBED BEN NEVIS.
Among the Bens.

75,000 FORDS FOR 1912

The challenge of climbing Britain's highest mountain by car was repeated by Henry Alexander in 1928 after the model 'T' had been replaced by the new model A. Incredibly he again met with success when the car used this time was SC 2328 seen here during its Ben Nevis climb. The model 'A' unlike its predecessor had a conventional 3 speed gearbox and four wheel brakes which were never available on the model 'T'. Not to be outdone in the same year another car reached the summit when George Simpson scaled it in SF 9917, a 'baby' Austin 7.

Many years later, at a motoring event in Edinburgh in 1954, the successful model 'T' of the 1911 Ben Nevis climb is seen with Henry Alexander and George Simpson (driving). This was a very much rebuilt version of the original and S 1871 had been appropriately named Ben Nevis as may be noticed on the bonnet. Other motoring attempts, not always successful, have since been made on the mountain including one by a group of medical students in an Austin Gypsy in 1962 and in a Land Rover the following year. In 1969 a Gnat defied the bogs, rocks and other obstacles to reach the top.

New in 1921 was ST 1755 which was one of three model 'T' hire cars based on the island of Harris and owned by Tom Cameron of Tarbert who is seen here at the Rodel Hotel. Tom liked his vehicles to be just that little bit different and had his three model 'T's re-painted from the standard Ford black to red, blue and khaki respectively, this one being khaki. Other non-standard features included the detachable Michelin wheels, the replacement cast aluminium radiator, the acetylene headlamps and the side screens, none of which were supplied originally. Tom can again be seen on p 103.

The Clachan of Strachur, Loch Fyne, in 1922 with two model 'T' Fords outside Montgomery's garage, the local agency. Due to the demand for model 'T's, these were left hand drive versions imported from Detroit, despite the fact that Ford had opened its Trafford Park factory in Manchester in 1911 where of course right hand drive models were produced for the British market. A Calthorpe 'Minor' sports model is in the foreground.

Ford's British factory moved in 1932 to premises in Dagenham, Essex, which are still used today. The first truly British Ford was the 8 hp side valve model 'Y' which was built there. FG 9328 and 9832 are four door examples of this model and are seen in St Andrews outside Forgan's shop in the Links (latterly St Andrews woollen mill) where it overlooked the 18th tee of the Old Course. R. Forgan & son had four similar Y types fitted with specially built felt-lined trunks to carry golf clubs. These cars dated from 1934 and cost £120 at that time but the following year the two door model became the first closed car in the U.K. to be sold at only £100.

This immediate post-war scene in now-pedestrianised Buchanan Street, Glasgow shows FXO 580 a London registered Ford Eight of 1939 pulling in to park. This model had developed into the Anglia, while the Ten became the Prefect. Behind the Ford is an Austin Ten of 1936 and it was quite possible that both cars had been laid up for the duration of the 1939-45 war, during which time many difficulties including fuel rationing conspired against the motorist.

In 1951 the 1½ litre four cylinder Ford Consul was introduced along with the larger six cylinder Zephyr. VHS 35 was one of the very last restyled model 375 Consuls, delivered in May 1962 shortly after final production. It is seen in snowy conditions later that year in rural Renfrewshire, home county of this car.

The Roaring Twenties

ARROL ~ JOHNSTON

THE Arrol-Johnston 13/30 h.p. "Victory" Car. PRICE, with Body, Hood, Screen, Electric Lighting and Starting, Detachable Steel Wheels, Spare Wheel and Tyre, Speedometer, Electric Horn, etc., etc., £700. . . . CHASSIS PRICE, £600, delivered at Works.

As far as the motor industry in Scotland was concerned, the decade which followed the Great War period lived up to its name, with several new Scottish built marques appearing. Some were to disappear as quickly as they had arrived but nonetheless trade seemed more buoyant than stagnant, giving a general air of hope to those involved.

Immediately after the 1914-18 war, Arrol-Johnston re-started car production in their Dumfries factory with what was sadly to prove a failure. Named the Victory to celebrate Britain's triumph in the war, this car proved so unreliable, despite many attractive and innovative features, that it was quickly withdrawn and replaced by what amounted to a revamped version of the pre-war 15.9 hp model.

The Arrol-Johnston Company extend to you the **Compliments of the Season** and trust that the suggestion contained in this advertisement may soon be realised.

Arrol-Johnston Ltd.

DUMFRIES.

"The Pleasures of Peace"

These drawings from a post-war Arrol-Johnston brochure show the pre-war model which quickly replaced the ill-fated Victory in 1919. This was also the only model believed to have carried the A-J initials as a radiator badge on the grille. The historic location of this scene is Courthill Smiddy, Keir by Penpont, Dumfriesshire, where local blacksmith Kirkpatrick Macmillan built the first bicycle around 1840. Artistic licence has included this beside the Arrol-Johnston.

A similar situation took place with the first of John Brimlow's revived Argylls in the post-war period which, like the Arrol Johnston was also based on their 1914 model, but without the pre-war refinement of four wheel brakes which explains why Argylls had previously been ahead of many rivals. SB 34 was registered in Argyllshire and had originally been allocated to an Argyll taxi in 1906 then re-issued in March 1920 to Argyll Motors when the company had returned to the Bridgeton factory. This was a 15/30 hp open tourer used as a demonstration model and is seen at the junction of Burnside Road and Upper Bourtree Drive in High Burnside.

One of the new Scottish built cars to appear after World War I was the Gilchrist designed by Sam Gilchrist of Giffnock and produced in premises in Govan. Bodywork was by Sim and Wilson of Cathcart and power was provided by the same 11.9 hp Hotchkiss engine used in contemporary Morris Cowley cars. Success eluded the Gilchrist and the company closed around 1923.

Royal Scottish A.C. Reliability Trials
JUNE 5———JUNE 10, 1922.

RECORD !!

The

8·10 hp.

ROB ROY

covered

the course

of

1020

miles——

WITHOUT ANY ENGINE STOPS.   WITHOUT ANY ASSISTANCE ON HILLS.

WITHOUT USING ANY   WITHOUT USING ANY WATER.

      LUBRICATING OIL.   WITHOUT ANY TYRE TROUBLE (Dunlops)

1st on Average Hill-climbing Results for whole week.

1st on Cairn o' Mount.

1st on Speed Test.

1st on Petrol Consumption

(Heaviest Car in its Class, yet did over 40 miles per gallon).

PRICES:

De Luxe Model **£325**   Standard Model **£295**

ALL DETAILS ON APPLICATION.

The KENNEDY MOTOR CO., Ltd.
SHETTLESTON, GLASGOW.

Other Scottish cars of the same period included the Scotsman produced by J. Hall Nicol in Wigton Street, off Possil Road, Glasgow in 1922/3 which was not to be confused with the car of the same name built in Gorgie Road, Edinburgh in the final years of that decade. The Glasgow built car, with its thistle shaped radiator, was often known as the 'Flying Scotsman' and the entertainer Sir Harry Lauder, who was also a keen motorist, reputedly had a financial interest in the company. The car shown in this advert from 1922 was another whose name immediately betrayed its Scottish origins. This was the Rob Roy built by respected Glasgow engineer Hugh Kennedy at his Koh-i-noor works in Shettleston. Previously he had been responsible for the Ailsa car (see p. 99). Many Rob Roy cars were bodied in Keppochhill Road by Norfolk coachworks, who also bodied the first two motorbuses (Commers) for Glasgow Corporation in 1924.

Thomas Charles Pullinger of Arrol-Johnston decided to build a light car based on the popular Fiat Tipo 501 and accordingly set up a separate company to do so in 1920 named the Galloway Engineering Co. Ltd., with a base at their former aero engine works in Tongland, Kirkcudbrightshire. Manager at the factory was Pullinger's daughter Dorothée and the majority of the workforce was also female. A 10.5 hp car originally known as the Queensbury but quickly re-named the Galloway was manufactured here until 1922 when production was transferred to Arrol-Johnston's Dumfries factory. A Coventry registered example of a Tongland built Galloway two seater is shown. This was proclaimed as the first car in Britain to be sold for £100. It was not until the middle of the following decade that Ford made the same claim for their enclosed 8 hp Y type two-door saloon.

Arrol-Johnston's factory at Tongland, Kirkcudbrightshire was purpose built during the Great War to produce the 13 hp Pullinger aero engines for the Air Ministry. It is seen as it was between 1920 and 1922 when Galloway cars were built there by a mainly female labour force, some of whom are visible. Facilities for the employees were first class and even included a tennis court on the roof.

Caught by the camera at Glasgow's Kelvin Hall motor show in 1923, after production of the Galloway car had been transferred from Tongland to the parent Arrrol-Johnston works at Dumfries is a 20 hp two seat coupe with manageress Dorothée Pullinger at the wheel demonstrating the controls to prospective purchaser Miss Mona Vivian.

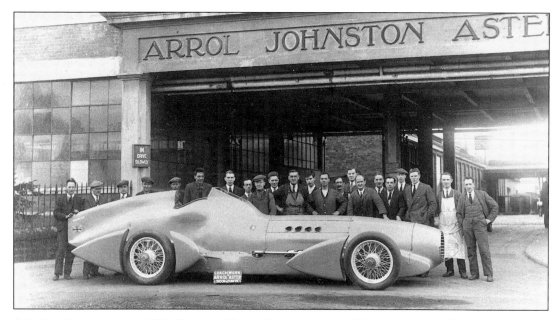

At the Dumfries factory in late 1927, after Arrol-Johnston had amalgamated with car and engine makers Aster of Wembley, we see the Napier engined Arrol-Aster 'Bluebird' with some of the workforce outside the Heathhall works where the body had been constructed. The following year Sir Malcolm Campbell set a new speed record with this car at Daytona, Florida, at a speed of fractionally below 207 m.p.h.

Both the Arrol-Johnston and Galloway names were dropped by the new company in 1928 in favour of consolidating under the Arrol-Aster title to focus on marketing luxury cars. A depressed period in Britain was certainly not the best time to do this and perhaps inevitably the company went into voluntary liquidation during 1929. However, Arrol-Aster continued to produce a further small number of cars while in the hands of the receiver until 1931 when the doors finally closed on the motor industry in Dumfries. An example of an eight cylinder Arrol-Aster 23/70 saloon is seen crossing Brig' O' Turk in the Trossachs area of Perthshire. The UX registration indicates the car was new in 1929 to an owner in Shropshire.

17/50 h.p. ARROL-ASTER
6-Cylinder Coachbuilt Saloon £598

A contemporary Arrol-Aster advert from 1929 which clearly shows the stylish Aster-designed coachwork on this 17/50 model. During their relatively brief production, Arrol-Asters gained a fine reputation for both comfort and reliability.

One of the best-known names in engineering in the Glasgow area was Beardmore whose company founder Sir William Beardmore was Lord Invernairn of Flichity, Inverness-shire who was involved in an amazing variety of engineering, transport and other interests. In 1919 car production started in three separate factories: the Beardmore 'Eleven' was built at the firm's Temple Works in Anniesland; the 'Thirty' at their Speedwell Works in Coatbridge and taxicabs at the Underwood factory in Paisley formerly used by Arrol-Johnston. In addition, there was a workshop at Beardmore's Parkhead Forge which produced pressed steel frames for their automobiles. Beardmore cars achieved somewhat more success than other Scottish makes during the 1920s although they too fell by the wayside and production ceased by 1928. This contemporary advert for the light Beardmore 'Eleven' originally appeared in 1922.

BEARDMORE

The Car for Scotsmen

¶ Made in Glasgow.

¶ Factory Service always available.

¶ Spares immediately supplied.

¶ Best value for your money.

¶ Buy a Beardmore and keep your countrymen employed, and Scottish money in Scotland.

**Stand
No. 54
Scottish Show**

Two-Seater -	**£475**
Four-Seater -	**£495**
"Sports" Two-Seater -	**£550**

BEARDMORE MOTORS LIMITED
LIGHT CAR WORKS :: ANNIESLAND, GLASGOW

BEARDMORE

Beardmore taxicabs and small buses were built at Underwood Works in Paisley where the associated Arrol-Johnston company had produced cars before their move to Dumfries in 1913 and where during wartime the factory had produced high explosive shells. In 1919 the first of many cabs appeared from Paisley known as the Beardmore Mk I and were particularly popular on the streets of London. They were of the landaulette type with three passengers facing and two sitting back to the driver. Cost of this 4 cylinder 16 hp model was then £650. Later, Beardmore Motors of London continued to make taxis until 1969.

Frank Menzies of Conon Bridge was a talented engineer who ran a small garage in that Easter Ross village. It was perhaps an unlikely location for motor manufacture but over the 2 decades between 1927 and 1947 he built four light three-wheelers including a small truck. JS 2920 was the first of the Menzies cars (the letter M badge is visible on the radiator) and was powered by a 3 hp Villiers 2-stroke engine which drove the single rear wheel by chain via the Sturmey Archer 3 speed gearbox. The extended kick start is visible protruding from below the plywood body which had been built by the village joiner and cabinetmaker Kenneth MacKenzie. Nevertheless this 'home made' car was belied by its professional appearance which was equivalent to that of many factory products.

The final Menzies car was JS 8973 in 1947 with single wheel at the front and again using a Sturmey Archer gearbox but with a Levis 2-stroke engine which proved underpowered because of the heavy sheet steel bodywork.

American automobiles have been popular in Britain since the birth of motoring and during the 1920s the big six cylinder models particularly so. One of the best known manufacturers in the United States was Buick which had a very Scottish connection because David Buick originally hailed from Arbroath before emigrating and producing his first car in Detroit in 1903. This illustration shows GB 5156 which was a Buick tourer of 1924 seen near the summit of the 'Rest and be Thankful' hill road which climbs through Glencroe en route from Arrochar to Inveraray. The main dealer for Buick cars in the Glasgow area was the Western Motor Co. of Berkeley Street.

Another Buick was this impressive left hand drive import from the USA which was a 1930 model seen in King Street, Stirling. Note the number plate QQ 9394, which was one of a special series issued to the Automobile Association for vehicles belonging to foreign visitors. Both the British AA badge and the American triple A badge may be seen on the radiator. Parked behind is a Morris Oxford traveller's van of the late 1920s.

Oakland was another American marque in the 'twenties, shipped across the Atlantic from Pontiac, Michigan. In the mid 'twenties import duty was increased in a largely unsuccessful attempt to stimulate the British market and stem the flow of these hugely popular imports from the USA although in order to circumvent this legislation certain US manufacturers used devious means to avoid paying penalties, such as Buick who had their British exports transported from a Canadian factory. This particular Oakland was shipped even further when it was purchased second hand by Leask of Lerwick in Shetland. SF 4007 worked when new in 1926 in Edinburgh, later passing to John Leask who operated it as a hire car, seen here at Reawick Hotel, Shetland. The cheaper Pontiac, also a General Motors product, ousted Oakland from the market and final production was in 1931.

John Leask of Lerwick operated both taxis and buses in Shetland. Two other examples of late 1920s American origin which joined his hire fleet were these six cylinder Chryslers from Detroit dating from 1928 but were second hand acquisitions by Leask, whose business today is still well known in the Northern Isles. Edinburgh registered SC 3055 on the left was a Chrysler '75' while PK 3819 was originally from Surrey and was a '70' model.

A Bullnose in the Borders. This Morris Cowley 2 seater with dickey was captured by the camera in the pleasant village of Town Yetholm in Roxburghshire where it was registered KS 3243 in 1926.

The 'Hungry' Thirties

. . . so called because of much economic distress during this decade, which saw the remainder of the dwindling number of Scotland's motor makers disappear, leaving only Albion Motors as an indigenous Scottish manufacturer (who had been concentrating on commercials since 1913.)

It is also interesting to record that the first edition of the Highway Code was published in 1931.

A street scene in the little Perthshire town of Comrie in 1931 looking from Dunira Street to Drummond Street, with Bridge Street to the right. The vehicles all date from the late 1920s and prominent in the foreground is Edinburgh registered SC 2280, a Rover 16 hp of 1928 with the badge of the Royal Scottish Automobile Club (which celebrates its centenary in 1999) on the radiator filler cap. On the other side of the street is GS 1586, a locally registered model 'A' Ford of 1929 while a Leyland Lion bus in the fleet of Walter Alexander of Falkirk heads towards Crieff having travelled via Strathyre and Lochearnhead on service from Callander. A sign hangs outside Brough & MacPherson's drapery on the left advising of their agency for the Castlebank Laundry of Glasgow.

Also in Perthshire, this view shows the popular village of Crianlarich as it was in the early 1930s. Situated at the junction of the road from Glasgow via Loch Lomond to Oban and Fort William and the route leading through Strath Fillan to Tyndrum it has always been a busy spot. Additionally it is of course a railway junction and this looks towards the railway viaduct and the road eastwards through Glen Dochart past snow-capped Ben More towards Killin. The cars are from the left, a wire-wheeled Standard '9' driving past a Morris Oxford flatnose, both from the late 1920s. A little Morris Minor is parked in the foreground while SC 9108 is a Fiat, both from 1930. Also visible is an Albion tour coach in the large fleet of Walter Alexander of Falkirk whose passengers were probably enjoying a break in Crianlarich Hotel to the right where their driver (with peaked cap) is standing.

43

GM 1550 was a Morris 15/6 fabric saloon of 1930 parked in Arrochar at the head of Loch Long outside Campbell Henderson's Teighness Hotel which burned down with tragic loss of life in the 1960s. The GM registration was a Motherwell and Wishaw issue.

A fine view of a six cylinder Austin with my initials which proves it to have been registered in the City of Aberdeen in 1931. This view in Orkney shows the light '12/6' RG 2337 leaving the old port of Stromness with the island of Hoy visible in the distance. The sliding sunshine roof was a common feature on most saloon cars of the period.

Another imported product from Detroit was this 3½ litre Hudson Super 8. GG 2575 was a 1931 example and is seen at the top of Buchanan Street in Glasgow advertising a daily public service to London in the comfort of its 7 seat interior. This was provided by motor agents Cameron & Campbell after the Road Traffic Act of 1930 as a speedier alternative to the bus services between the two cities which at that time took 16 hours. A similar Hudson is just visible behind.

The Scottish Motor Traction Company, more familiarly known as SMT was based in Edinburgh and had diverse interests apart from their core business of running bus services throughout Scotland. These included not only garage premises and automobile agencies but also a pleasure vessel on the River Forth and for a period in the 1930s an aircraft division. This scene is thought to have been taken at either Corstorphine or Turnhouse airfield in Edinburgh in 1932 on the occasion of chartered De Havilland Gipsy Moth aircraft being used to carry the 'Sunday Referee' newspaper for delivery in Aberdeen. The SMT-owned cars which brought the bundles of papers to the aircraft are a 15.9 hp Morris Oxford flatnose on the left and a Buick fitted with a radiator muff. The SMT diamond logo visible on the driver's door is still in use today.

Craignure on the island of Mull is the setting for this view outside the village inn. GG 6284 from Glasgow was a 14/45 hp Talbot tourer of 1932. Around this period Talbots were enjoying many racing successes but despite this the Sunbeam–Talbot–Darracq group was not in the best state of financial health and in 1935 Rootes gained control of the Clement–Talbot company which had been based in North Kensington.

RG 2783 was a 2 seater Morris Cowley tourer of 1932 with dickey (this was a folding seat at the rear for two extra passengers which was quite a common feature on 2 seat cars of the period and known as a rumble seat in the USA) It is seen in Gordon Street, Huntly, Aberdeenshire, with the town hall behind.

The Crown Hotel, Newton Stewart, was both AA and RSAC recommended as may be seen from the signs of both motoring organisations. The circular AA sign showing mileage to the next towns along the way is also afixed to the hotel wall, giving the distance to Wigtown as 7 miles. Leading the line of cars is FS 7628, a humble little Austin of 1933 with its owner checking below the bonnet. At the rear is US 7029, a brand new Humber of 1934 while in the middle and despite dating from the previous decade, this chauffeur driven Belgian-built Minerva is the most imposing of the three. Its registration G 26 suggests that its owner had transferred the Glasgow index mark from an early Edwardian vehicle owned previously.

OJ 6063 was a Birmingham based Wolseley of 1933, seen here in the main street of Pitlochry where it would appear that the driver had pulled up to seek directions from a local cyclist. This was the year when Wolseley introduced their famous illuminated radiator badge which was a trade mark for many years to come.

In the previous scene a cyclist seems to be having a conversation with the car's occupants while in this view the horse appears to be doing the same. The location here is Linkster in Shetland and the car is a Ford Ten Prefect of 1935. The YS registration letters were originally allocated to the Burgh of Partick before it came under the control of the City of Glasgow.

Popular with Scottish motorists was the 30 hp Ford V8. YS 1545 was a 1935 example seen in Argyllshire on the eastern shore of Loch Fyne at St Catherines.

Outside the golf clubhouse at Muirfield, East Lothian in the mid 1930s. AAO 226 is a Cumberland registered Riley of 1934 and the other car a Ford V8 Pilot.

Jedburgh High Street looking from the Spread Eagle Hotel towards the Mercat Cross in 1935 with a fine collection of vehicles from that decade. These include brand new Stirlingshire registered Rover WG 3884 on the left; YJ 2322 from Dundee, also new in 1935, was an 8 hp Ford Y type 2 door saloon which in that year became the first full-size make of car to be sold for £100. Driving towards the camera is FS 426, a 1931 Morris Commercial van from Edinburgh, while alongside it is KS 4742, a model 'A' Ford of 1930, locally registered in Roxburghshire.

Photographed in 1938 on board the ferry *Thane of Fife* which sailed across the Forth (see also p. 83) between Burntisland in Fife and Granton near Edinburgh is WS 9449, a 1936 Ford 10 and FS 7236, a Morris 12/4 of 1933, both of which were registered in Edinburgh. WS had been the index mark for independent Leith until 1920 when it was incorporated into the Edinburgh system on the city's amalgamation with the burgh that year.

Francis Street in the attractive West Highland village of Dornie, Wester Ross in the late 1930s. DKJ 61 was a 'Flying Standard', new in 1936 in Kent and probably brought north by a visiting holidaymaker.

It seems hardly credible that on the date of this photograph, 27 May 1938, the Esplanade of Edinburgh Castle was devoid of visitors and their cars. It is almost impossible these days to find a square inch between cars and coaches at this location, which is Scotland's main tourist attraction. The lone car on this occasion was WS 5830, which was a Morris 10 new in 1935.

Late 1930s in Langholm High Street, Dumfriesshire. On the left is CSM 545, a locally registered 12 hp Wolseley of 1937 and on the right KS 6763, an Armstrong Siddeley sports saloon of 1935 from Roxburghshire.

The ferry port of Stranraer, Wigtownshire in the late 1930s with OS 5002, a locally registered Rover 10 of 1938 making its way along Hanover Street.

The Solway shore at Rockcliffe on a warm summer day in 1939. Unknown to them at this time, it would be the last summer motorists could enjoy their cars with freedom as war broke out later that year and considerably curtailed pleasure motoring. The day trippers are out in force as we see from the selection of parked cars at this popular picnic spot. Austins predominate but in the foreground is a 1937 Singer Bantam and a Morris 10 is also visible.

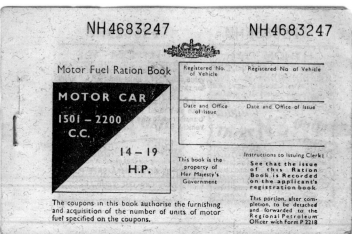

During the dark days of wartime between 1939 and 1945, Britain's motorists had little incentive to enjoy their cars and indeed many folks laid them up and did not take them out of mothballs to re-license them until hostilities ceased. Petrol rationing was inevitably introduced and it lingered in force until 1950 and was in fact resumed during the Suez crisis from late 1956 until summer 1957. Reproduced is an example of the fuel coupons required during rationing periods.

DFS 391, a Rover 12 which had been new in 1939, with radiator well muffled on this occasion to help combat the elements during a severe post-war winter. The snowy scene is just outside the borders village of Morebattle, Roxburghshire which had been home to Scotland's pioneer motorist Thomas Elliot (see p. 3)

Another scene to set you shivering. The old Devil's Elbow road through Glenshee between Blairgowrie and Braemar was formerly a much more difficult route (see p. 55) before its many severe gradients and zig-zag bends were ironed out with road improvements. CGG 888 was an attractive Morris 8 series E tourer of 1939 and this type only enjoyed a short production run since it was not built in post-war years. The photograph dates from May 1951 when the snow still lay deep but nevertheless the hardy travellers in the convertible have lowered the hood to enjoy the sun.

Highland Highways,
City Streets

This section includes a look at some of the rugged roads over which the intrepid early automobilists had to drive.

In a 1906 Scottish motoring journal, some roads were reported as being 'Oceans of glaury ooze'. Certainly an apt description in this instance of a road somewhere in Aberdeenshire in Edwardian days. The occupants would appear to have abandoned the comfort of their Albion 16 hp landaulette to allow the chauffeur to extricate it from the mire while the gentleman on the right attempts to assist by directing the driver with a lot of hand waving. Although this was north-east Scotland, prevailing road conditions at that time were generally similar everywhere.

One of the main entry roads into Scotland from the south is that which crosses the Cheviot Hills at Carter Bar en route from Northumberland (now the A68). MS 476 was a 20 hp Standard tourer of 1910 pausing for a photograph at the road sign then recently erected by the Scottish Automobile Club to mark the border into Roxburghshire. The affluent owners of this automobile have lots of luggage with them since not only is there a trunk strapped to the rear, another two are on the front seat beside the chauffeur. In early Edwardian days this route was not recommended to motorists because of its rough surface of loose stones and the alternative road via Coldstream was the preferred journey.

Between Pathhead and Carfraemill on the same A 68 main road south from Edinburgh another gradient must be surmounted in the shape of Soutra Hill (1131') in the Lammermuirs. A fine view of the Lothians can be enjoyed from here and this Edwardian group must have been doing just that when stopped near Soutra summit on a summer day in 1908. S 916 was an Edinburgh registered Austin 18/24 tourer.

In Edwardian times the drive from Blairgowrie to Braemar over the Devil's Elbow (the highest main road in Britain, reaching a height of 2,200' at the summit) was no mean feat, especially with its loose stony surface which may be clearly seen. Asphalt roads were then still mainly in the future. Rounding one of the severe hairpins encountered as it heads north towards the Cairnwell Pass and Braemar in 1909 is a 12/15 hp Paisley built Arrol-Johnston tourer.

'Leaving Loch Maree, June 1909,' is the caption on the back of the original photograph. A prominent family from the Scottish border country enjoyed some splendid touring holidays in the Highlands during Edwardian times and in 1909 their itinerary included the drive along the shores of Loch Maree, between Kinlochewe and Gairloch, Wester Ross. At that period this road was euphemistically defined in motoring guides as 'inclined to be soft.' Today's superb road by the lochside could almost be described as a motorway in comparison to its condition 90 years ago. The car which tackled so many daunting roads during this family tour was KS 109 a new 18 hp Wolseley Siddeley, seen here with protective covers over the side and headlamps which not only prevented stone damage from the loose road surface but assisted the brasswork against tarnishing. The next scene depicts the following year's Highland Tour with the same car.

A pioneering example of Motorail! Some of the early railway companies shrewdly offered transport on their wagons to motorists who wished to escape the hazards of some of the more difficult sections of road. The North British Railway for instance provided such an alternative between Crianlarich and Fort William, thus avoiding the drive through Glencoe and across Ballachulish Ferry, both of which were more of an adventure than a pleasure drive in the Edwardian era. The scene here was at Strathcarron station in Ross-shire where the Highland Railway offered rail travel for automobiles to Strome Ferry and Kyle of Lochalsh with ferry connections for Skye. This obviated the necessity of driving along the north side of Loch Carron through Jeantown and Slumbay and then crossing the loch by the Strome ferryboat which in any case actually cost more than putting the car aboard the train since the rail freight charge was only 7/6d as compared with the 10/- ferry fare! A drive to Kyle over indifferent roads then followed as there was no route along the south side of Loch Carron until the Strome Ferry by-pass road opened fully in the early 1970s.

One can almost smell the smoke and steam in this atmospheric view which was caught on camera on July 15, 1910, when another tour of the Highlands was enjoyed by the same family from Roxburghshire (see also previous view) in their Wolseley/Siddeley tourer KS 109. For those with interests in the iron road, the locomotive was Highland Railway no. 88 which was one of the Skye Bogie class built in the company's own Inverness workshops around 1895 and remaining in service until 1926.

In 1912, one year after his successful publicity drive to the summit of Ben Nevis in a model 'T' Ford (see p. 30), Henry Alexander attempted another motoring feat in a model 'T' but on this occasion was unsuccessful. He set out to drive the full length of General Wade's old military road built in the 1730s across the Corrieyairack Pass from Dalwhinnie to Fort Augustus but had to admit defeat with about a quarter of the route still to complete shortly after Mealgarbh, the location of this photo. The car was registered ST 312 in 1911 to Patrick Vernon Chinnery-Haldane of Onich, who was presumably one of the doughty travellers. Another passenger on the trip was author and historian J. Inglis Ker, who mentions the attempt in one of his contemporary travel guides. Ker was also at that time editor of the Glasgow-based magazine *Motor World* which remained in weekly publication until the late 1960s.

The 20 hp model 'T' Ford was a rugged little car which coped admirably with our equally rugged roads and quickly gained popularity in Scotland where local depots were soon set up to attract further custom. The Ford agent serving the Orkney islands was W.R. Tullock of the Orkney Cycle & Motor Depot in Kirkwall who supplied these two examples prior to the 1914–18 war. They are seen near Marwick Head on an outing to the Birsay area of Mainland. Model 'T' Fords were originally built in the Detroit suburb of Highland Park and of course Orkney is home to the Highland Park whisky distillery, providing an interesting link.

Feshie Bridge, Invernessshire, crosses a gorge over the River Feshie a little east of the village. This road (now the B970) provides a quiet alternative on the east side of the Spey to the main route between Kingussie and Grantown on Spey. ST 200 was an Overland landaulette, a product of the Willys -Overland Co., of Toledo, Ohio. This was new in 1914 to Ewan Campbell & Son, garage proprietors of Main Street, Kingussie, who enjoyed good trade by hiring cars and drivers to affluent visitors at the various local shooting lodges. The business later passed to Joseph McCormack of Kingussie.

Essex cars were built by the Hudson Motor Car Co. of Detroit, Michigan. V 6594 was a touring example of this make from the very early 1920s, licensed in Lanarkshire and seen here on the rough surface of the High Street in the west coast fishing port of Mallaig (steam herring drifters may be seen in the harbour) where at that time transport links were provided primarily by rail and sea. The only road, which climbs steeply from the village towards Arisaig and ultimately onwards to Fort William was then in an extremely poor state and daunting to all but the hardy (or foolhardy).

The hill road which leads from Arrochar at the head of Loch Long to Inveraray on Loch Fyne climbs to reach nearly 900' at the summit known as Rest and Be Thankful. This was originally a drove road for cattle but was repaired and upgraded by the military in 1768 as part of the plan for the pacification of the Highlands. This mid 1920s view from the top shows the road in the valley below climbing through Glen Croe. In the late 1930s construction commenced on the present more direct road which takes a course above the original and this was opened in 1945 after wartime delays. The signpost points left to Cairndow and St Catherine's and right to Arrochar, while the Sunbeam tourer is parked at the junction with the Lochgoilhead road, which was described in an Edwardian guide book as being no better than 'a rough cart track'. Today this location may still be seen in the view-point area just off the main A 83 highway.

Another road which could only be described as a cart track was high above Loch Leven in Invernessshire and was a segment of General Wade's old military route to Fort William (now part of the West Highland Way.) The occupants of YN 5794, a 1926 Armstrong Siddeley tourer from London enjoy the view across the loch towards the P ap of Glencoe from the Mamore side. The hill rising behind the car is the Cailleach, or old lady.

On the island of Lewis in the 1920s the west side road through Valtos Glen in the Uig district was rough and stony. Posing there for a picture in a brand new 1926 Citroen were Norrie McIver with his wife Nan and father-in-law Donald McAulay, who was a well known draper and general retailer in Stornoway.

A former cattle drove road which was described variously in the mid 1920s as 'not very good', 'dangerous' and 'terrible' ascended Mam Ratagan between Shiel Bridge and Glenelg in Invernessshire, from where you can still sail 'Over the Sea to Skye' by the summer only Kylerhea ferry and thus avoid the toll on the Skye Bridge. The dramatic roads on either side of the ferry crossing easily compensate for the detour and justify taking this route. Back in the 'twenties on the mainland side this Morris Oxford 'Bullnose' was captured on camera as it cautiously climbed towards the 1100' summit from sea level at Shiel Bridge with a glorious view overlooking Loch Duich below.

Looking towards the Atlantic Ocean from the road between Durness and Tongue along Scotland's far north coast in the late 1920s. The scene is at Rispond near the entrance to Loch Eriboll and the car used by the ladies was YH 2851, a London registered Daimler 20 hp tourer new in 1927.

At the other extremity of the country YN 9624, also from London, was an Alvis 12/50 of 1926 at the 1371' border summit of Carter Bar in Roxburghshire on a journey from Edinburgh to Newcastle. The photo was taken in 1930 by which time the road had been improved from its former state (see p. 55) and widened which allowed service buses to operate between the two cities.

Although this photo was taken in 1936, the roadway may be seen to have a loose, stony surface. Even after the 1939–45 war certain streets and roads in many counties did not have the benefit of an asphalt covering and accordingly caused dust problems for adjacent householders. This view looking towards the Kilpatrick Hills shows Greenhead Road in the Silverton area of Dumbarton, with a message boy struggling up the gradient on his delivery tricycle while working for Templeton the grocer. The cars are HS 8343, a Standard 10 of 1935 and a distant Y type Ford 8.

Roads on Scotland's islands were generally of a reasonable standard, although naturally tended to be single track since the volume of traffic did not justify otherwise. As the years progress this is becoming more of a problem and upgrading has brought an increased mileage of double width roads which has not necessarily pleased everyone. The Isle of Skye is an example of this, where the greater number of vehicles has been encouraged by the Skye Bridge, despite the high toll charges. This view at the north end of the island in the late 1950s shows PNN 822, a 1954 Ford Consul with visitors from Nottingham squeezing past the service bus from Portree to Uig and Kilmaluag operated by MacLeod of Duntulm, whose driver has taken to the verge. WG 9834 was a wartime Bedford OWB utility model which had originally entered service with Alexander of Falkirk in 1943.

Motor traffic in Scotland's four cities and also several towns including Ayr, Dunfermline, Greenock, Kilmarnock, Kirkcaldy and Perth had to compete with the electric tramcar for road space. To be fair, the trams had usually been the first to arrive and in any case the local municipalities paid for the upkeep of the portions of the streets used by tramways; nevertheless the resultant congestion was occasionally even worse than now. This late 1920s scene was photographed from what is now the Sauchiehall Street bridge across the M8 motorway at Glasgow's Charing Cross. A tram turns from St George's Road at Charing Cross Mansions into Sauchiehall Street ahead of a queue of westbound trams heading towards the junction. The motor cars (Glaswegians usually referred to their trams as cars and to cars as motors) were both 14/40 Talbots, the saloon in the foreground being AG 2277 while parked at the kerb (no restrictions then) and thus adding to the congestion was tourer RA 2348, both new in 1927.

Buchanan Street in Glasgow was not served by the tramway system and thus perhaps benefited from freer flowing traffic more than most other streets in the second city. Looking from St Enoch Square northwards in the early 1930s we see a variety of transport including a horse-drawn cart heading towards us and a porter pulling a hand cart laden with trunks no doubt from the nearby St Enoch railway station. The cars include GE 2571, a 1928 Vauxhall on the left passing SM 8193, an Austin 7 of 1930. Crossing the tramlines in Argyle Street is an Austin heavy 12 followed by a Sunbeam and a Morris Commercial. Samuel's corner has only recently become part of Fraser's store after having been a city landmark since 1901 when the jeweller's opened during the September week of the car trials at the Glasgow International Exhibition (see p. 97).

A later view of Buchanan Street looking north in 1933. Parked outside Fraser's store is AG 4452 a Daimler 15 of 1929, while passing by is HS 6892 a 1932 sports Humber followed by a Morris Oxford saloon. The fashionable ladies are spoilt for choice with Fraser's, Jaeger and Wylie Hill's all adjacent and Miss Cranston's restaurant just a little way further.

Glasgow's St Enoch Square almost had the appearance of a huge parking lot when this scene was captured in the mid 1950s. Today of course it is a pedestrianised zone with the huge St Enoch shopping centre occupying the former railway station site on the right. The numerous cars visible date mainly from the 1940s and '50s and include an Austin Atlantic, Ford Zephyr, Hillman Minx, Jaguar, Jowett Javelin, Riley, Rover and Wolseley to name but a few. The buses include a couple of Corporation double deckers (one with 'L' plates for trainee drivers), a Lowland Motorways AEC Regal and outside the air terminal on the right is one of the Commers with Harrington 'dorsal fin' bodywork used by BOAC to connect with their flights at Prestwick Airport.

The north side of St Enoch Square in the late 1950s, looking towards the junction of Buchanan Street and Argyle Street, where a Corporation tramcar passes Samuel's corner. Younger folk may not remember the information bureau where the Gap store now stands, nor for that matter some of the cars of the period. These include a Standard 8 of 1954, a split-windscreen Morris Minor of 1953, a Ford Prefect of 1955, a 1933 MG, a 1950 Sunbeam Talbot and a 1937 Austin. The taxi on the left is a Beardmore while the bus is a Leyland Tiger new in 1940 to Western SMT and has just pulled around the corner from the stance in North Drive at the start of its journey to Largs via Renfrew. The British Railways poster advertises dining car excursions to the Grand National at Aintree for only 40/- (£2) return from the adjacent St Enoch Station.

A late 1930s view looking west from Union Street, Aberdeen's main thoroughfare, where it meets Holborn Junction ('Babbie Law'). Driving towards the camera is locally registered RG 8212, a Wolseley 'big 6' of 1937, while a Ford Y type is parked on the 'wrong' side at the pedestrian crossing where a group of people cross at the Belisha beacons towards Chivas' family grocery store on the corner. Adding to the general interest of this scene is a city-bound single deck Albion bus in the Corporation fleet passing one of the municipal tramcars heading for Bridge of Dee.

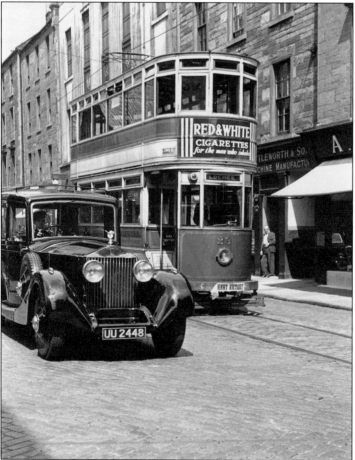

At the opposite end of Union Street shortly before withdrawal of the Corporation tramway system in 1958. The overhead wiring may be seen at the junction of King Street and Union Street where Aberdeenshire registered OAV 529 heads across the tramlines. This was a Morris Minor of 1957 being followed through the junction by two Weymann bodied AEC double deckers which belonged to Aberdeen Corporation. Garthdee-bound DRG 485 was a 1949 example and BRS 519 behind dated from 1946.

UU 2448, a Rolls Royce hearse originally registered in London in 1929 but seen a quarter of a century later in Dundee passing a Corporation tramcar on the Lochee service in Lindsay Street near its junction with the Overgate. The last trams in this city of jute, jam and journalism as it was at that time ran in 1956.

Motor cars competed for road space with tramcars in our capital city until 1956. This scene in Princes Street looking towards Calton Hill was taken from the top of Waverley Steps in 1935 when the Corporation trams were in their prime. An Essex registered model 'Y' Ford of 1933 leads a 1925 Dodge delivery van past the trams picking up passengers outside the North British Hotel (now the Balmoral). Today only west-bound traffic such as this is allowed in Princes Street and this too is threatened with a ban, to permit only public transport in Edinburgh's principal thoroughfare.

One year later this view was taken from the opposite side of Princes Street looking towards the North British station hotel with visitors' cars in the foreground. BVU 50 to the left was a 1935 Manchester registered Wolseley while VV 2072 from Northampton was a baby Austin Seven of 1933 parked outside the Old Waverley Hotel with what would appear to be the owner's suitcases on the pavement. A puff of exhaust smoke on the other side of the street betrays one of a fleet of Leyland Titan double deckers which had been delivered in 1929 to the SMT fleet based in Edinburgh and seen leaving the bus stance at Waverley Bridge as one of the city tramcars passes bound for Granton.

Smaller Scottish towns such as Gourock in Renfrewshire also had tramcars on the streets, the owners in this instance being the Greenock and Port Glasgow Tramways Company who operated local services in the Inverclyde towns until 1929 when this view was taken in Shore Street looking towards the pierhead from opposite the Municipal Buildings. Prominent is GB 5401, a Morris Cowley 'Bullnose' of 1924 with a model 'T' Ford and a Daimler bus of the early 'Twenties visible outside Gourock's 'Kursaal' which housed a roller skating and ice rink and dance hall. The Bay Hotel and the Post Office were later built on this site, but both of these have now also been demolished for redevelopment of the area.

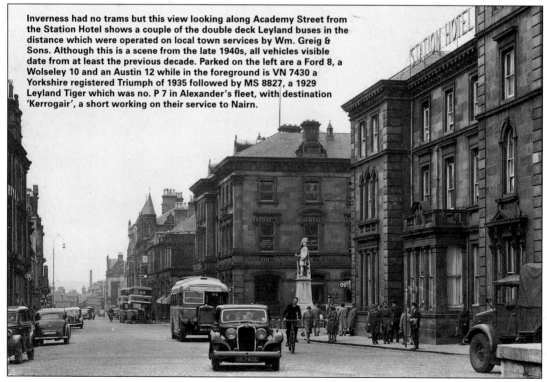

Inverness had no trams but this view looking along Academy Street from the Station Hotel shows a couple of the double deck Leyland buses in the distance which were operated on local town services by Wm. Greig & Sons. Although this is a scene from the late 1940s, all vehicles visible date from at least the previous decade. Parked on the left are a Ford 8, a Wolseley 10 and an Austin 12 while in the foreground is VN 7430 a Yorkshire registered Triumph of 1935 followed by MS 8827, a 1929 Leyland Tiger which was no. P 7 in Alexander's fleet, with destination 'Kerrogair', a short working on their service to Nairn.

Inverness again but this time looking along High Street from the Castle Street junction in 1952. A Ford Y type of 1934 is parked outside Woolworth's with a pre-war Vauxhall heading past. Driving towards the camera is CST 636 a 1948 Austin 16 registered in the county and followed by a local haulier's Albion lorry, while the nose of an Austin pokes out of Castle Street. This scene today is of course very much changed since pedestrianisation of the High Street.

Aftermath of heavy snowfall in the early 'fifties near the Borders village of Morebattle, Roxburghshire. (see also p. 53) The local roadmen had only shovels to carry out the clearing job in those not so far-off days before county roads departments employed less labour intensive but more sophisticated methods such as motor snowploughs. Just visible and waiting to be rescued is a British Road Services breakdown wagon which had no doubt set off on a rescue mission itself before becoming trapped.

A classic street scene from September 1955 showing Methil High Street in Fife, looking towards the Palace cinema and the post office beyond. Cars include FDA 862 a 1947 Austin 10 from Wolverhampton, NFG 96 a local Morris Cowley of 1954 and NSP 331 a new Morris 'J' type. The children on the right are hovering with their mum outside the confectioner's where a notice reads 'freshly made ice cream sold here' while Thomson the butcher stands in his doorway. It is generally unknown that Methil was planned as the location for what could have become one of Scotland's most important motor works. In 1906 local landowner and far-sighted industrialist Lord Randolph Wemyss of nearby Wemyss Castle intended to purchase British manufacturing rights for Mercedes and construct these high quality cars at Buckhaven. Sadly he died before final agreement was reached or we may have seen Fife-built Mercedes and thereby possibly retained a motor industry in Scotland.

Another mid 1950s scene which also depicts an Austin 10, but despite its identical appearance to the 1947 model in the upper photo, DGB 804 dated from 1940. Austin simply resurrected this pre-war design once hostilities ended and sold them just as successfully with the post-war demand for cars far outstripping supply. The location is Renfrew Ferry at the terminus of the Glasgow Corporation Tramway service from Paisley which was withdrawn in 1957. Coronation type tram 1280 leaves for Glenfield, followed by Standard 147 for Lochfield Road while additional interest is provided by the tug D. Waterston and a Riley car whose radiator is hidden by the suicidal pedestrian attempting to catch the departing tram.

Camping and Caravanning

A caravan holiday in the Scottish Borders in the late 1920s. Car, caravan, tent, teapot and dogs are all here with father and family in a farmyard at an unknown location. The Morris Oxford Bullnose of 1926 has the Newcastle on Tyne registration number TN 1447 indicating that the group was from that area. The caravan was possibly of Eccles manufacture.

An early example of a mobile caravanette was SF 7660, with a purpose-built body on Morris Commercial chassis. It is seen during its first season on the road near Beauly while touring the Highlands in the summer of 1927. The owner was a Mr. Lawson who owned a drapery business in Dundee.

Another instance of a mobile home built on a commercial vehicle chassis was this 2-ton Bedford WLG of 1933 which had the appearance of a double deck bus and was completed with beds for six, a fitted kitchen, bathroom and even a bar. It was then undoubtedly the grandest caravan in Scotland and is pictured with its builder and owner, Peter Crerar of Crieff, seen chatting to McGregor the postie outside Leadenflower Road coachworks (now a supermarket) where many charabancs had been built by Crerar for his own touring company in addition to orders for other customers. Peter was also proprietor of the cruise vessel *Queen of Loch Earn* and the Crieff cinema but surprisingly despite the publicity at his disposal the caravan was exclusively for personal use and was not offered for hire.

More conventional cars and caravans are seen in the late 1930s on the site at Ganavan Sands by Oban, a holiday location once favoured by Scotland's favourite family 'the Broons'. In addition to the local bus bringing day trippers to the beach, the cars include a Ford 10, a Vauxhall big 6, a Morris Minor and a Morris 8.

Another popular caravan site was that which overlooked the East Sands at St Andrews, seen here in August 1955 with VS 4465, a Greenock registered Austin Eight of 1946 looking out to the North Sea.

A caravan with a difference was this one in use as a mobile bank with the Royal Bank of Scotland during the 1950s when several such units were operated in rural areas. Powerful cars were obviously required to tow such heavyweights, in this instance JXJ 768, a 6-cylinder Humber Super Snipe of 1949.

Cars and Ferries

Ferries in Scotland have provided important transport links since centuries before the coming of the motor car. With the birth of the automobile, ferries soon benefited from increased business although initially were ill-equipped to do so as they were slow to adopt motor power themselves. Especially on our Atlantic west coast which is deeply indented by sea lochs, ferries have saved many weary miles of road travel and of course throughout the Northern Isles and Western Isles ferries have always been part of the local scene, interconnecting the smaller islands and also providing links with the Scottish mainland.

Although now exceptionally safe, ferry crossings are often still regarded as a bit of an adventure. In the early days of motoring this was particularly true as is evident from this view of a Paisley built 1902 Arrol-Johnston car on the ferry at Ballachulish where it was not until 1912 that a motor vessel replaced the original rowing boat. Because of the swift current here the ferry was often pulled well downstream before struggling across the narrows which was a tribute to the strength of the crew. This car is similar to that on p.11 but unusually was fitted with a canopy and curtains to keep the sun from lady passengers during trips to the south of France made by the owner, Barclay Harvey, MP of Dinnet House, Aboyne, Aberdeenshire. The 'Surrey with the fringe on top' was a 6-seater which was later registered SA 3 in 1904 once licensing was introduced.

Ballachulish Ferry was one of the best known in Scotland, used over the years by many thousands of Scots and visitors alike as it shortened the west coast journey to Fort William and the far north by avoiding the considerable detour around the head of Loch Leven. Now but a memory, it ceased operation on the opening of Ballachulish Bridge in December 1975. On this occasion in the late 1930s the car about to leave the *Queen of Glen Albyn* at the south side was Berkshire registered AMO 342, a two litre MG of 1937. These initials stood for Morris Garages, a name synonymous with lively sports cars.

The crossing at the narrows of Loch Linnhe is made by the Corran Ferry over to Ardgour from where a mainly single track road leads to the westernmost extremity of mainland Britain at Ardnamurchan Point, beyond the village of Kilchoan. This mid sixties view from Corran on the Nether Lochaber shore shows the council operated ferry in mid stream with one of the remaining members of a once large family of Maudslay Marathon buses from the late 1940s in MacBraynes fleet waiting to provide the connecting service for Fort William. The cars include Morris Minors, a Mini, a 1962 Hillman Minx and a 1963 Mercedes 220.

Eilan Donan Castle makes a splendid scene from the old ferry pier at Ardelve, Ross-shire. Often known as the Aird Ferry, it sailed to the village of Dornie over the mouth of our northern Loch Long until the crossing was bridged in 1940 thus providing a quicker journey to Kyle of Lochalsh and the next ferry along the route to the Isle of Skye. On board is a Belgian built Minerva two seat tourer with dickey dating from around 1930.

'Over the Sea to Skye' between Kyle and Kyleakin in July 1927. Balanced somewhat precariously on two planks and projecting over both sides of the ferry is a Rolls Royce charabanc during a 5 day tour of the Western Highlands and Skye provided by pioneer coach company Rankin Brothers of Glasgow which was the first to advertise Scottish motor coach holidays in the United States. Rankins purchased a number of second hand Rolls Royce limousines in the mid 1920s and had the chassis lengthened by Mechans engineering works in Scotstoun with 12 seat charabanc bodies built by Cadogan of Perth for use on tours which incorporated ferries and narrow roads inadvisable for larger vehicles.

Two of the Skye ferries during the late 1940s. *Cuillin* is about to cast off with its two car maximum load from the jetty at Kyle of Lochalsh on the mainland side while its sister vessel has arrived from Kyleakin on Skye and disembarks a motor cycle combination and a 1946 Ford Anglia (EWS 122). With the opening of the toll bridge at this crossing point in October 1995 the vehicle ferries latterly operated by Caledonian MacBrayne were withdrawn.

For today's motorists who may be determined to cross to Skye by ferry, there are still two alternatives to the bridge. Caledonian MacBrayne operates between Mallaig and Armadale in the Sleat district of south Skye while a privately owned summer seasonal sailing crosses the narrows from mainland Glenelg to Kylerhea. This ferry is pictured on the Skye side in the summer of 1938, with two cars led by an Austin arriving for the steep and rough climb which awaited them through Glen Arroch before reaching the main island road to Portree. The light coloured saloon waiting to board was BGT 446, a 1934 Bentley from London which was fitted with 'GB' plates.

Before the road along the south side of Loch Carron was built, motor traffic had to use the Strome Ferry if travelling from Inverness to Kyle via Achnasheen or the railway service when it was available (see p.56). Here we see the ferry 'Strome Castle' at the south landing in September 1959 with a Messerschmitt 3-wheel bubble car (built between 1953 and 1962 by the former German aircraft company) first to disembark, followed by a 1955 Austin A40 Devon and then a tour bus. This was a 29 seat Alexander bodied Albion 'Nimbus' of 1957, a small lightweight model with underfloor engine which was used on touring duties by David Lawson of Kirkintilloch, a member company of the erstwhile Scottish Bus Group. Strome Ferry was withdrawn in the early 1970s when the new road opened linking Strathcarron with the A87 Kyle/Invergarry road at Auchtertyre.

The ferries of David MacBrayne and predecessors (now Caledonian MacBrayne) have been indigenous to the Western Isles for generations. Prior to the introduction of car ferries into their fleet in the early 1960s any motor vehicles heading for the islands usually had to be slung on board by a winch, as seen here at Mallaig where a Vauxhall Cresta PA series of 1960 swings in mid-air before landing on the deck to join other cars on board MV *Lochmor* which sailed on the outer islands mail service to the Uists and Harris.

Cars destined for the Island of Mull were ferried from Oban on the mainland by MacBrayne vessels as deck cargo before the arrival of purpose built car ferries. This scene at Salen on Mull, which is no longer served by ferry, dates from 1936 and shows FG 5502 a 10 hp Swift 2 seater of 1929 vintage driving from the pier to the deck of the daily mailboat *Lochinvar* for conveyance to Oban which of course was a manoeuvre totally dependent on the state of the tide. The object behind is not a caravan but the top of the pier shed. The car was named 'Rosinante' by its owner Peter Macnab of Tobermory and latterly West Kilbride, who has written several books about Mull.

The attractive port of Tobermory on the island of Mull as seen from a MacBrayne mailboat departing the pier in the late 1950s with a Ford Prefect and Austin Cambridge among the cars. Piers were always focal points for locals and visitors alike who would gather to enjoy the bustling atmosphere at boat time. The functional yet agreeable Art Deco design of MacBraynes pier buildings of the 1930s are also recognisable at other Hebridean locations such as Port Ellen on Islay and Stornoway on Lewis. The village of Craignure on Mull and not Tobermory was chosen as the main island link when the large car ferries were introduced from Oban in the 1960s, although a smaller car ferry connects Tob as it is familiarly know locally with Mingary on the Ardnamurchan peninsula.

Kylesku Ferry provided the link across the head of Loch Cairnbawn in north-west Sutherland on the road between Inchnadamph and Scourie and it was thanks to the efforts of the Royal Scottish Automobile Club that the first car ferry was introduced at this crossing in 1923 (built by Dickie Bros. of Tarbert, Loch Fyne) In later years while under control of Sutherland county council this was the only free ferry in Scotland, both pedestrians and vehicles enjoying this privilege until 1975. The vessel continued to operate until July 1984 when Kylesku Bridge opened with the inevitable withdrawal of the ferry service. This mid 1950s scene from Kylesku Hotel at the south landing shows the approach of the ferry *Maid of Kylesku* for a Ford Prefect (CTS 827) and a Morris Minor van (AJS 691) both dating from 1953.

When is a ferry not a ferry? The answer is when its Connel Ferry Bridge. The ferry which crossed the mouth of Loch Etive between North and South Connel was eventually withdrawn due to insufficient business after the railway branch line between Oban and Ballachulish opened in 1903. After the ferry ceased, if motor traffic wished to cross then initially drivers had to load their vehicle on a special railway wagon between Connel and Benderloch, or vice versa, although an alternative did exist by using the Bonawe Ferry further up the loch near Taynuilt, which mainly served the

Bonawe quarries on the north side. From 1912 it was possible to use the narrow stretch of roadway alongside the railway line over Connel Bridge outwith train times and this arrangement continued, albeit with a toll charge, until the line finally closed in 1966. Once the tracks were lifted the roadway across the bridge was widened but nevertheless remains a one-way system controlled by lights. This photo was taken by the driver of the Fiat open tourer in the foreground and shows traffic queuing to cross at the south side in 1928. The warning sign reads 'ONE WAY TRAFFIC. DO NOT MOVE WHEN GATE IS OPENED UNTIL INDICATOR CHANGES FROM 'STOP' TO 'COME ON'. RING BELL AND WAIT.'

Several ferries catering for both pedestrian and vehicular traffic crossed the River Clyde from those in the city of Glasgow down to that between Old Kilpatrick and Erskine. One of the oldest established was Renfrew Ferry, crossing from that Royal Burgh to Yoker on the north side of the river. This scene from 1936 shows a chain-driven steam ferry at Yoker looking across towards the now removed electricity pylon after which the former adjacent Paton Bros. bus depot was named Tower Garage. Leaving the ferry is XS 3748, a Paisley registered Austin 10 of 1935 followed by FG 8360, a 1933 model 'Y' Ford from Fife. The two commercials aboard are a late 1920s Albion and a 1931 Ford 'A' van owned by the Gleniffer Laundry of Paisley but strangely with the Belfast registration AZ 8239. In 1984 the last of the chain ferries was replaced by passenger only vessels which currently still serve this crossing.

Down-river from Renfrew, there was a similar chain ferry linking Erskine in Renfrewshire with Old Kilpatrick in Dunbartonshire. This was withdrawn when Erskine Bridge opened in 1971, much to the relief of many motorists who particularly during the summer months had to endure lengthy queues for the crossing. This was a typical scene in August 1962 when the Dormobile driver faced a wait of at least two hours before boarding since this location at the Bishopton road junction was ¼ mile from the ferry. Prominent in the foreground is UGB 371, a 1958 Austin FX3 Glasgow taxicab alongside a motor cycle combination of the Automobile Association whose patrol man keeps a watchful eye on the frustrated ferry queue, which lengthened each successive year until the bridge opened. The AA Scottish headquarters now occupies a site not far from the former Erskine Ferry.

When the River Clyde widens to become the Firth, ferries become even more important. A slipway was constructed at the north end of Cumbrae to accommodate the introduction of car ferries in 1972 which sailed from Largs on the Ayrshire coast. TSM 498T, a 1979 Volvo Estate leaves the Caledonian MacBrayne vessel *Isle of Cumbrae* for the 10 minute drive to Millport, the only town on the island.

Ferries were always fewer on Scotland's North Sea coast because the east side of the country has no sea lochs like its Atlantic counterpart. Today apart from the Nigg Ferry across the mouth of the Cromarty Firth no east coast ferries remain because of bridge building programmes over the years. This illustration shows the Kessock Ferry which plied between North and South Kessock across the narrows linking the Beauly and Inverness Firths. The late 1940s scene shows a big pre-war Austin Twelve saloon accelerating from the *Eilan Dubh* up the pier on the Inverness shore while passengers board to cross to the Black Isle beyond, after which the vessel was named in Gaelic. When Kessock Bridge opened in 1982 the ferry became redundant.

The Tay ferry *Scotscraig* approaches Newport pier in Fife during the mid 1950s. On the north side of the Firth of Tay the unmistakable outline of Dundee Law is clearly seen looking down on the former jute city. Makes of cars waiting to join the ferry include Triumph Roadster, Wolseley, Ford and Hillman. The Tay ferries, familiarly known to Dundee folk as 'the Fifies', became a memory on completion of the road bridge in 1966.

Yet another vehicular ferry which ceased with the opening of a bridge was the historic Queensferry crossing over the Firth of Forth between North and South Queensferry in Fife and West Lothian respectively, named after Queen Margaret of Scotland who journeyed by this route between Edinburgh and Dunfermline in the 11th century. Sir William Arrol's mighty Forth railway bridge, opened for traffic in 1890, dominates this view of Hawes Pier at South Queensferry in 1929 when the American Buick saloon was brand new. The Forth road bridge replaced the ferries in 1964.

An often forgotten ferry was that which sailed across the Forth between Granton on the Edinburgh side and Burntisland on the Fife shore. The service tended to be intermittent over its chequered history and after a brief two year revival the final year of operation was 1952 from which time there has been no vehicular ferry. An Austin Sixteen is seen on board the drive-on vessel believed to be *Bonnie Prince Charlie* at Granton Harbour in the early 1950s. In pre-war years another ferry company had operated a similar service with the vessel *Thane of Fife* from 1937 until 1940.

Garage glimpses

Pioneer Glasgow motor agents Rennie & Prosser represented Angus-Sanderson, Arrol-Johnston, Crossley and Panhard cars in the city. From earliest days they operated a vehicle recovery service and this photograph from 1905 shows their Milnes-Daimler breakdown lorry which contemporary publicity claimed to be 'fully adapted and equipped for motor ambulance work'. This of course was not meant to imply that it carried the sick to hospital but disabled automobiles to Prosser's garage seen here at 60 North Wallace Street.

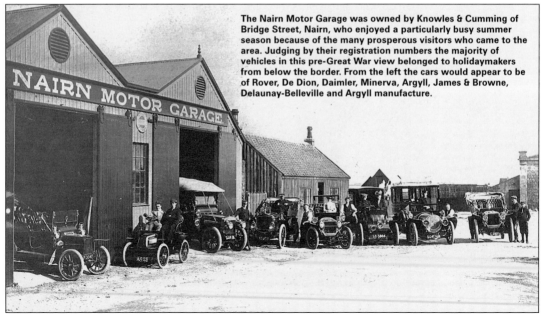

The Nairn Motor Garage was owned by Knowles & Cumming of Bridge Street, Nairn, who enjoyed a particularly busy summer season because of the many prosperous visitors who came to the area. Judging by their registration numbers the majority of vehicles in this pre-Great War view belonged to holidaymakers from below the border. From the left the cars would appear to be of Rover, De Dion, Daimler, Minerva, Argyll, James & Browne, Delaunay-Belleville and Argyll manufacture.

An Edwardian garage scene, believed to have been the interior of the premises in High Street, Cowdenbeath occupied by the Beath Motor Co. All vehicles carried the local Fife 'SP' plates. SP 1175 and 1146 were both model 'T' Fords, while the make of the charabanc SP 1202 is unknown, although the name of its bodybuilder is clearly visible on the original print as Smith & Son of Larkhall, Lanarkshire. The trend at that period was for owners to give their charabancs names and this one was R(h)oderick Dhu, from Sir Walter Scott's epic *Lady of the Lake*, albeit wrongly spelled by the signwriter.

Because most early automobilists were necessarily amongst the more affluent members of society, garages were often provided at superior hotels for the benefit of motoring guests, sometimes in addition to and sometimes replacing earlier stables as the horse steadily gave way to the ever increasing number of motor cars. This scene from 1913 shows ladies on the balcony of the National Hotel in Dingwall, the Ross-shire county town, looking down on examples of both forms of transport. A top-hatted coachman is in charge of the horse and carriage, while the horse enjoying the flavour of the hotel hedge is pulling a local dairyman's cart. This hotel remains much the same in appearance today but the local war memorial now stands where we see the 'motor garage' sign.

Whyte Brothers' Strathmore Garage in the Wellmeadow, Blairgowrie, shortly after they took over the premises from Roderick Rait in 1922. Alf Whyte and Dick Farquharson started the business which quickly expanded from motor repair and engineering to also include the operation of bus services from Blair to Dunkeld, Bridge of Cally and Perth. This line of their vehicles includes hire cars, taxis and a charabanc as follows; Overland S 5087; Humber with no visible plate; Lancia charabanc ES 4104 (named Fair Helen); Belsize SA 1294; Singer SA 1412; Benz SR 567.

The owner and the location are unfortunately not confirmed other than somewhere in Glasgow but nevertheless this scene from 1922 provides a fascinating glimpse into a garage. The cars on the right are both Standards including GA 2303. To the left and carrying trade plates is an Amilcar 'petit sport', which as the name suggests was a sporty voiturette from St Denis in France. Also from France was the La Buire from Lyons which is partly hidden by the garage foreman standing in front. Because of the French connections it may be that the premises were those of the grandly named Glasgow and Paris Motor Garage and Repairing Co. Ltd., in Avenue Park Street, Maryhill, who were also agents for Berliet and Delahaye cars and Michelin tyres.

Two scenes at Invergordon in Ross shire showing Taylor's garage which was originally in Clyde Street as seen in the pre-1st World War view with KT 854, which was a 12 hp Rover registered in Kent and SU 332 a French Clement-Bayard. The mid 1920s view shows their newer garage in the High Street with ST 3569, an Inverness registered model 'T' Ford receiving attention (Taylor was the local Ford agent) and a newly erected Pratt's petrol bowser in the foreground.

A country garage in the early 1920s. This was Robert Anderson's Ford agency in the village of Pirnmill on the west coast of the Isle of Arran. He also owned the local shop and tearoom and in addition operated a charabanc service to Lochranza in connection with steamers to and from the mainland. A couple of the ubiquitous model 'T' Fords peep through the garage door and of course all the placards are for Fords, that on the left advertising the Fordson tractor for £205.

The first purpose-built petrol service station in Edinburgh was erected in 1922 by the Peebles Motor Co. Ltd. at their site in Russell Road and naturally attracted much favourable publicity at the time since this was a great advance on the tedious alternative of filling from two-gallon tins. A Sunbeam tourer fuels up from the bowser which took its name from S.F. Bowser & Co., who introduced the petrol pump into Britain in 1913.

The equivalent first petrol station in the Glasgow area did not come until a few years after Edinburgh's and surprisingly only survived for a relatively short time since business here was to prove quieter than anticipated. The location in question was in Thornliebank at the 'Jenny Lind', which was the name given to the area at the junction of the Stewarton and Paisley roads and named after an inn on the original site. The owner of this purpose-built filling station was Humber and Armstrong Siddeley agent Robert Anderson whose main workshops were in Newton Mearns, with another garage in Giffnock. Parked at the pumps which promote Shell and Benzole is a 14 hp Armstrong Siddeley fabric saloon known as the 'Four 14' which was their last model before the famous pre-select gearbox was introduced in 1928 and also one of the few with a flat radiator as opposed to the usual V shape.

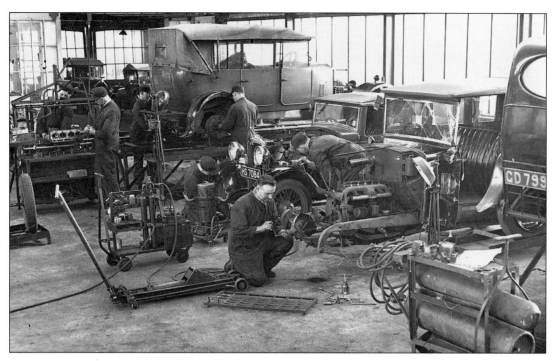

Hard at work in Anderson's garage at Newton Mearns in the mid 1930s. On the right and up on ramps is GD 7990, an Alvis 12/50 sports saloon of 1928 with large oval rear window. Next is what would appear to be a Morris Cowley flatnose probably in for accident repair judging by its shattered windscreen; then we see HS 7084, a 1933 Crossley Ten built in Manchester by a company which concentrated solely on their commercial vehicle output from 1937 onwards. On the ramps is a 20 hp Humber from the previous decade with a similar car just visible in the shadows at the back. Anderson's business had included an agency for Humber pedal cycles in late Victorian times which naturally progressed into a Humber motor dealership with the advent of the early automobile and continued as a Rootes Group main dealer until the closure of the company in 1980.

The garage in the grounds of the huge private estate owned by His Grace, the Duke of Buccleuch at Drumlanrig Castle, Dumfriesshire in the mid 1920s. The 24 hp Albion bus in the centre was new in 1923 and was mainly used for transportation of guests to and from the railway station at Thornhill. It is flanked by two of the four Rolls Royce Silver Ghosts owned by the Duke; R 1064 registered in the county of its birth, Derbyshire, dated from 1911 while Dumfriesshire indexed SM 328 was a 40/50 hp landaulette of 1908 which had been returned to Rolls Royce at Derby for modernisation including the fitting of this later, taller type of radiator.

Two views which compare the Edinburgh Corporation Transport Department car fleets in 1926 and 1931, both inside their Central Garage in Annandale Street and both featuring Morris Cowley cars, which found favour with the Edinburgh municipality. The earlier scene shows mainly SG and SF registered Cowleys of 1924 and 1926 respectively, which were all of the famous 'Bullnose' type of that period. Amongst some of the other makes of car in the back row are Rover, Austin and Wolseley. The 1931 view shows newly delivered Cowleys with numbers in the FS series which arrived via local agents the Westfield Auto. Co. of Gorgie and ousted the early models. Each one sports a radiator badge featuring the Edinburgh City coat of arms.

A typically Scottish small town garage scene from the late 1920s. These were Finlay Dickson's premises in Rigg Street, Stewarton, Ayrshire in 1929 with the family living quarters above. He was a Ford agent and here we see AG 4120, a brand new apple green model 'A' Tudor (two door) along with proprietor Finlay Dickson himself accompanied by his son John and not forgetting Fido. Also noteworthy is the Pratt's 'Ethyl' petrol bowser which swung out from the wall and just decipherable on the sliding garage door is a circular AA road sign for Stewarton, showing distance to Kilmarnock as 5 miles and Dunlop 2½. Latterly this was McFadzean's garage but was recently demolished to make way for redevelopment.

An equally typical country garage scene from a decade later. This was the corrugated iron A. & M. garage (nowadays Purvis Hill garage) in the Borders countryside on the edge of Walkerburn, Peeblesshire, with the River Tweed in the valley below. The petrol pumps gave the choice of Shell, Cleveland Discol, National Benzole or Redline and as we see, it was not uncommon for the local smith to share garage premises where he often also assisted with motor maintenance. The horse being shod would appear to hold more interest for the children than LS 3580, the attractive little 2-seater Morris 8 convertible of 1935.

A 1938 scene inside the College Street garage of Elgin Motors which today is a supermarket but at that time was controlled by the SMT group. The cars in the foreground are SO 6398 and 5776, both Wolseley 14s of 1938 and 1937 respectively and RG 7087 a 1936 Morris 10. To the rear are Armstrong Siddeley DVK 430 of 1936 and SO 5708, a Humber Snipe of 1937. Sharing the garage in the background we see some of Alex. Hay's buses which operated local services from Elgin to Pluscarden, Forres and Covesea.

Mention the name Taggart around the Motherwell area and it will probably be associated with the well known local garage rather than the TV detective series. James Taggart had originally served his time as an engineer with Hurst, Nelson & Co., the tram and railway wagon builders in Motherwell and then opened a cycle shop in Brandon Street in 1897. Natural development involved the new-fangled automobile as the 20th century dawned and by 1910 Taggart Bros. were agents for Arrol-Johnston and Darracq cars. A peep inside the old established premises at Knowetop after the restrictions of the 1939–45 war reveals a mid-thirties Austin Six saloon with Lanarkshire registration number VA 77 originally issued in 1922, indicating that this was a cherished plate no doubt re-issued to subsequent cars of its original owner. On the ramps is GM 3732, a Motherwell & Wishaw number on a new 1946 Austin Ten which was presumably snapped up quickly since demand for cars far outweighed supply in the post-war years.

The Joys of Motoring

Despite problems from an ever increasing volume of traffic on our roads and spiralling fuel prices coupled with regular road tax increases, there are few of us who would willingly give up their car. The automobile could perhaps be described as an extension of one's home in many respects, with the relative privacy this brings while travelling in one's personal capsule. The joys of the open road can be as exhilarating today as they were in Mr. Toad's Edwardian era assuming everything runs smoothly, but when it doesn't . . .

Since the pioneering days of the first primitive automobiles breakdowns have resulted in frustration and often family friction too. Caught by the camera near Galashiels in 1905 is a 12 hp De Dion Bouton which was a popular import from France. However, this one was causing problems for its owner who is seen in a rather unflattering pose beneath the bonnet. Meanwhile his well-dressed wife waits patiently in the rear seat of the tonneau possibly musing on Robert Louis Stevenson's words, 'To travel hopefully is a better thing than to arrive. . . .'

Collisions naturally caused grief but at least there were no fatalities from this accident in 1914 at the Birnam road junction just across the River Tay from Dunkeld. The signpost points left to Birnam, Murthly and Perth and right to Aberfeldy while an additional roadsign has been erected by the SAC (Scottish Automobile Club) which indicates that Crieff is 22 miles distant and Carlisle 155. This particular contretemps took place between Perthshire registered ES 1806 of 1914 which was an almost new model 'T' Ford and SP 1670, a 1912 Darracq with Fife registration. The inevitable swarm of spectators, many in military uniform, clusters around, but no sign of the constabulary as yet.

The poor condition of many of our roads in earlier years was such that punctures were relatively commonplace and so most motorists were quite adept at changing wheels and pumping up tyres. An example of just such an incident on the island of Lewis in the mid 1920s occurred in the Tolsta district on the north east coast and involved JS 1596 which was a 1924 Overland. This car was built by a subsidiary of Crossley Motors called Willys Overland Crossley Ltd. of Stockport which was set up to assemble cars in Britain for the American parent Willys Overland Co. of Toledo, Ohio. The gentlemen seen here were well known in Lewis at that time since T.B. McAulay on the left was a gent's outfitter while Duncan McIver was a fish curer.

An accident near Dale on mainland Shetland in the late 1920s when this Ford was ditched. SA 6048 was an Aberdeenshire registered model 'T' which had been new in 1923 and fitted with a proprietary ribbed radiator which replaced Ford's own. This was the year when production of the model 'T' peaked with an incredible two million built. The view from the rear shows some of the effort required to get the 'Tin Lizzie' back on the road. Although these cars were usually disparagingly known by this and other equally derogatory terms they were in reality sturdy little vehicles well suited to our rugged roads as testified by the large numbers sold.

A road in rural Renfrewshire was the scene of this early 'thirties collision involving two elegant saloon cars from Glasgow which both dated from 1931. GG 5216 was a Vauxhall Cadet while GG 4052 was an Alvis Silver Eagle which had probably been supplied by Galt's of Glasgow, the main dealer. The Coventry-built Alvis was fitted with a Wilson pre-select gearbox which was also incorporated in the heavier Crested Eagle which remained in production after the Silver Eagle was dropped in 1936. Rover obtained a controlling interest in the company in 1965 and two years later Alvis cars ceased production.

The Loch Lomondside road was one to be treated with caution and respect for many years until its relatively recent major improvements, which even now have not yet reached the northern section. This scene from the early 1960s shows the fate which befell a 1956 Vauxhall Victor whose impatient driver had attempted to overtake on one of the many blind bends on the old road. The tour coach which he met head-on was a new Bedford/Duple Bella Vista in the SMT fleet.

Trials and Competitions

As we are a naturally competitive race, trials have been held to assess the endurance of both car and driver virtually since the dawn of motoring. The earliest such major event was that organised in 1900 by the Automobile Club of Great Britain and Ireland (now the Royal Automobile Club) and known as the 1000 miles trial which consisted of a tour lasting 3 weeks from London to Edinburgh and back. Its object was to demonstrate to a curious public the capabilities of motor vehicles over long distances and hopefully stimulate the demand for cars to the benefit of the then fledgling motor industry in this country. Out of 84 entrants, 51 survived the first half of the trial to Edinburgh and were on show to the Scottish public in Waverley Market on May 3rd 1900. This scene shows some two-seaters leaving Edinburgh from where they headed south through Haddington and Dunbar for the border at Berwick along what is now the A 1 road. A New Orleans (built in Twickenham despite its name) heads the line followed by a French De Dion and an English International. No Scottish-built cars took part.

The first major public motor car trial to be held entirely in Scotland was also organised by the Automobile Club of Great Britain and Ireland. It took place in September 1901 during the Glasgow International Exhibition at Kelvingrove. For the first time ever, many people took the opportunity to examine at close quarters and marvel at the up and coming wonder of the dawning century—the automobile. The 500 miles reliability trial consisted of a 5 day event covering a daily run of approximately 100 miles from Glasgow to Edinburgh, Ayr, Callander, Glendevon and Tyndrum and the participating cars were exhibited each day during the event at the new Gilmorehill sports arena which had been constructed on the University athletic ground, the location of this photograph. Prominent beside the starter's flag is a 10 hp Wolseley with well-respected Glasgow motor agent Harry Prosser standing alongside (in cap). Next is a 7 hp Panhard/Levassor with Mrs. Prosser seated inside, followed by a 4 hp Stirling/Benz described as a Parisian phaeton (built by John Stirling in Hamilton).

The official printed instructions to the competitors included the following caution aimed at the many entrants from England; 'Drivers who are accustomed to driving in the south are reminded not to overlook the fact that the horses in Scotland have not yet become accustomed to motor vehicles and are apt to swerve and back their vehicles across the road to the great danger of other road users.' During my research for this book I discovered that amongst the well-known motoring names of the time who drove in this trial were Charles Jarrot, Cecil Edge, Harvey du Cros, The Hon. Charles S. Rolls and a Mr. Clarkson! Perhaps a relative of Jeremy?

Undoubtedly the most important motoring events in Scotland during the early days were the 4 and 5 day reliability trials organised by the Scottish Automobile Club which took place annually from 1905 until 1909 and initially set out to show that a motor car could travel anywhere its main rival the horse could go and without the time consuming preparations involving the animal. These trials always included taxing hillclimb sections and this scene during the 1907 event shows XS 53, a Paisley-built 38/45 hp Arrol-Johnston awaiting starter's orders at the foot of the Rest and be Thankful in Argyllshire followed by an American 30 hp White steam car and a French 40 hp Berliet.

'The motor car went poop-poop-poop as it raced along the road . . .' Thus wrote Kenneth Grahame in his Edwardian tale *Wind in the Willows* featuring Mr. Toad the original road hog, who would surely have enjoyed the atmosphere at the Scottish trials. A cloud of dust hangs in the air behind DU 1491 which was a 20 hp Rover entered in the 1907 reliability trial by their Glasgow agent James Gibbon. It has climbed Glen Croe and now approaches the hairpin bends towards the Rest and be Thankful summit. After the new road up 'the Rest' was opened in 1945 motor sport events continued to use the former route but owing to the poor state of the road today this is no longer permitted.

The Rest and be Thankful was obviously an ideal location for good action photography of the competing cars and this view shows an Ailsa 15/20 hp car built in Glasgow by Hugh Kennedy who later manufactured the Rob Roy (see p. 36). The Ailsa was one of 15 Scottish cars amongst the 104 entrants in the 1907 trial and carried Glasgow registration number G 233. It is interesting to compare the large capital letter A which formed the Ailsa radiator badge with the similar badge design of the Volvo-engined Ailsa double deck buses produced at Irvine three quarters of a century later. The following car was a 16 hp Bell built by Bell Bros., of Ravensthorpe, Yorkshire between 1905 and 1914.

In the 1908 Scottish Automobile Club reliability trial one of the hill climb events took place at Fintry in Stirlingshire and this scene shows a line of cars waiting to climb over the Campsie Fells in the final section heading back to Glasgow. Because of the very wet weather throughout most of that summer trial, the occasion looked more like the launch of a lifeboat than a motoring event. The sou'wester clad figures were all competitors and WS 34, the 1905 De Dion 10 hp car on the left was owned by an Automobile Club official as may be seen from the sign on its windscreen.

The last of the early major Scottish Automobile Club reliability trials was the six day event which took place in June 1909. DU 1926 was a 16 hp Humber starting off on the Glendoe hill climb outside Fort Augustus on the Whitebridge road. It had been entered by G.A. Phillips of Coventry and since its selling price was £388 was in category E (£325–£425) for trial purposes. The highest group was class H for cars between £650 and £800 which only applied to an English Ariel and a Belgian Germain.

Raising the dust as it approaches the summit of Cairn O' Mount on the Fettercairn to Banchory road in Kincardineshire after the long climb from Clatterin' Brig is a 10.5 hp Tongland-built Galloway during the first and only Scottish light car trials organised by the Royal Scottish Automobile Club in 1922. Note the presence of the official observer in the car, which was one of the pre-requisites of entry.

Naturally no motoring trials took place during the first World War but there was a resurgence of interest in the 1920s and this scene shows a line of competing cars and motor cycles during the Scottish 6-days trial in 1923 which had been organised by the Edinburgh & District Motor Club since the Edwardian era and still takes place today. The location is Ordiequish Hill, on a side road between Fochabers and Mulben in Morayshire and the line is led by K.W.B. Sanderson driving OK 5998, a Birmingham-built Ariel closely followed by HP 5480 which was an Albatros from Coventry and driven by a Mr. Brookes. Both Ariel and Albatros enjoyed the brief boom for light cars which peaked around this period but neither marque survived beyond the mid 1920s by which time business had fallen dramatically.

One of Scotland's most eminent engineers was Sir William Beardmore who had been with Arrol-Johnston in Edwardian days and whose wide range of interests included not only motor manufacturing but also aero engines, aeroplanes and airships. Apart from the solid and somewhat staid Beardmore cars and taxis (see p. 39) there was a high performance model produced at Anniesland from 1922 from which was developed this sports version. The scene here shows Cyril Paul breaking the Shelsley Walsh record in 1924 with an overhead camshaft 2-litre Beardmore.

Scottish Sporting Car Club events by their very nature provided some sticky situations for competitors and spectators alike. One such occasion was in March 1935 at Costerton near the Fala Dam, Midlothian when because of heavy overnight rain the going got tough through the mud. The assistance of extra horse power was obviously the required remedy and helped to get HS 39 back into the competition. It was one of several 'Anderson Specials' built by motor engineer James Anderson of Newton Mearns and carried the registration of his original Humber car from Edwardian times. They all enjoyed success at these sporting occasions and were usually driven by Robert Anderson. A later Anderson Special is now displayed in the Glasgow Museum of Transport.

Another incident which caused consternation occurred during a Scottish Sporting Car Club event in 1936 when Leslie Bisset was forced to abandon YS 6491, his new MG 'PB' in the Endrick Water while attempting to cross Drumtian Ford, near Killearn. Leslie, a well-known competitor in such events at that time, was forced to accept a 'piggy back' in order to reach dry land, assisted by appropriately named Mr. Playfair of Auchterarder.

The Cowal was completed in Drymen, Stirlingshire by engineer James W. Robertson in 1933 where it was registered WG 1990. It is seen being put through its paces with Robertson at the helm during the Scottish Rally of 1934 on the old Devil's Elbow road in Glenshee. Robertson's own two stroke V4 single sleeve valve 728 cc engine which he hoped to market was fitted to this one-off sports car. The engine survives as an exhibit in Glasgow's fine transport museum.

The first Monte Carlo Rally to start from Great Britain was in 1924 from Glasgow with sole entrant Frenchman M. Ledure (who was to win the rally) in a Bignan car. The following year it again started from Glasgow and then in 1926 the first start from John O' Groat's was made with an AC car driven by the Hon. Victor Bruce. This illustration shows no less a personality than Miss Amy Johnson who in 1930 had become the first woman to fly solo from England to Australia and who entered the Monte Carlo Rally from John O' Groat's in 1936. She is seen during this event refuelling her British 22 hp Ford V8 Pilot at Chapman's Garage in Inverness assisted by Thomas E. Cameron of Tarbert, Harris, who was garage manager at that time. Incidentally during a conversation with Tommy in 1990 when recalling this occasion, he assured me that his cigarette was not lit and also remembered that sadly Amy had skidded off the road near Pitlochry, writing off the Ford along with her chances of rally success but fortunately escaping serious injury herself.

K.W.B. Sanderson was a well known Scottish motor sportsman who had graduated from motor cycling to motoring events. He participated in the Monte Carlo Rally on several occasions including 1936 with this splendid 3½ litre Bentley/ Vanden Plas. CLA 811 was first registered in London in 1935 and is seen here preparatory to entering 'the Monte' from Glasgow with Mr. Sanderson and his co-driver Alfred Fourcroy of Brussels. An earlier scene on p. 101 shows Sanderson at the wheel of an Ariel during the Scottish 6 days trial in 1923.

The official starter in Glasgow at that far off original Monte Carlo Rally in 1924 was A.K. Stevenson of the Royal Scottish Automobile Club who later became Secretary and General Manager of that august institution. In fact 'A.K.' as he was usually familiarly known became somewhat of an institution himself in Scottish motoring circles. He is seen here in his 85th year at the start of the 1972 Monte Carlo Rallye as A.K. always correctly spelt it with complete accuracy. He flags off car 37, a Ford Escort, from outside the RSAC Clubhouse in Glasgow's Blythswood Square, which had been his home and workplace for so many years.

During the 1939 RSAC Scottish rally brake tests were carried out in the grounds of Taymouth Castle, Kenmore, Perthshire. Seen at this location was Keith Elliot, another familiar name in pre-war motor sport who was at the wheel of EHP 782 a brand new works-entered Triumph Dolomite roadster.

SSCC programme featuring F. R. Gerard in his E.R.A.

The Scottish Sporting Car Club hosted some very popular speed hill climbs which were inaugurated in 1934 over a course high above the Firth of Forth in the grounds of Kinneil Estate at Bo'ness, West Lothian. These continued in post-war years through to the 1950s and this scene from the late 1940s shows Alex. Reid of the Southern Cylinder Grinding Co., Glasgow in FGB 4, his BMW special, better known as 'Omega' which he had built himself. Many whose names were later to become almost legendary competed at Bo'ness, including a teenage Cooper expert called Stirling Moss.

The first outing of the Bentley driver's club in Scotland took place in March 1953 and included SG 4636 amongst the cars taking part, seen here at Newhouse Hotel. This had chassis no.19 and engine no.20 and was one of the original production 3 litre 15.9 hp models of 1921. At the time of this meet the car was still very original, fitted with rear wheel brakes only and polished aluminium bodywork by Gairn of Annandale Street, Edinburgh. Its owner and driver was Wm. Dale who later owned the former Motor Museum in Melrose.

A contemporary advert from 1950 featuring a caricature of Clement Attlee (Britain's first postwar Labour Prime Minister from 1945–51) driving an Austin while in a Bentley is wartime coalition leader Winston Churchill who ousted Attlee in 1951 to serve a further term as Conservative Prime Minister.

Another successful 'special' at post war motor sport events was the Rover-based Girastro (Gibbon, Ramsay, Starling, Rover) constructed in the late 1940s by Jim Gibbon and friends of his Glasgow family company which held the agency for that make. The car was originally built using mainly salvaged components including the chassis from a 1939 Rover 12 and engine built up from a 1940 Rover 10 but various performance enhancing modifications were carried out later. This scene during an early 1950s event shows a crowd of spectators on the hillside watching Jim Gibbon in command of the Girastro on the approach to the top hairpin of the old Rest and be Thankful which was formerly a popular motor sport course but now disused.

A Bo'ness speed hill climb in June 1954 for class 1 racing cars from 501 to 1100 cc with Ken Wharton who went up the steep, twisting course in a 996 cc Cooper in 33.76 seconds. Wharton was then holder of the course record with a time of 33.61 seconds made in June 1953. Below, he is seen again in a BRM.

At Fairmilehead in Edinburgh in September 1954 during the Anglo-American car rally sponsored by the British Travel & Holidays Association to help attract American tourists to Britain. Escorting the procession which had started from Edinburgh Castle is a 1949 Mk V Jaguar which was a popular choice of patrol car for many police forces at that period, followed by XU 362 the Alvis driven by rally organiser and transport historian L.T.C. Rolt. Then come the American entries headed by a 1906 6 cylinder Ford model 'K' Speedster and a 1906 20 hp Stanley steam car of a type advertised in the USA as a 'gentleman's speedy roadster'.

One of the most famous hill climb cars ever was Basil Davenport's GN 'Spider'. Davenport was a legend in his own lifetime having set a record three years in a row in 1926–7–8 at Shelsley Walsh and later making an incredible post-war comeback with this same twin cylinder, 2 litre special which dated from the early 1920s. This view clearly shows the car's almost razor like bonnet as it speeds around a hairpin on the Rest and be Thankful course during a competitive event in July 1955 in which Davenport achieved second in his class. A banner in the background advertises that year's forthcoming motor exhibition at Glasgow's Kelvin Hall.

Motor Shows

Scotland's earliest shows which featured automobiles were organised by cycle dealers, many of whom later became motor agents as the car struggled initially to gain even reluctant acceptance amongst the public. The very first show to include the motor car took place in Edinburgh's Waverley Market (now the site of the modern shopping mall) in 1897 with the grand total of four on display.

The majority of the early motor shows were held in Edinburgh although Glasgow was the venue in 1901 (at the International Exhibition) in 1906 at the Dennistoun Exhibition Hall and in 1907 at West Princes Street Drill Hall. Outside the Dennistoun venue in Duke Street in 1906 are from the left a French De Dion, an Arrol-Johnston from Paisley and an American Winton (Alexander Winton is largely forgotten in Scotland but was born in Grangemouth before emigrating to Cleveland where he built the first truly successful car in the USA) At the helm of the De Dion is John Smart Matthew of Dunlop tyres who was later to become managing director of Argylls Ltd. at Alexandria. The cup in the centre was presented to John S. Napier as the winner of the first Isle of Man tourist trophy race in 1905 in an Arrol-Johnston of which company he was managing director.

A 12/16 hp Sunbeam on delivery to the 1912 Scottish Motor Exhibition in Glasgow which was held at the Industrial Hall in Kelvingrove Park. Horse drawn wagons were still the most common means of haulage at that time and so, strange though it may seem, conveyance by this method was not considered an indignity. The faint outline of Glasgow University on Gilmorehill is just visible through the Autumn mist beyond.

Scottish motor manufacturers such as Argylls Ltd. regularly attended motor shows throughout the land and were also very publicity conscious. This advert for their display at the 1909 Olympia Exhibition in London appeared in various journals of the time and the artist has given an impression of Argyll cars speeding away from their palatial Alexandria factory in the background watched over by a classical beauty proving that the female form is nothing novel in car advertising. Note also the equally significant wording with a vague hint of something perhaps a shade risque, 'Range of Beautiful Models, 1910'.

Pictured at the same Scottish Motor Exhibition of 1912, held at the Kelvingrove Industrial Hall, is the stand where Robert Anderson of Newton Mearns displayed Armstrong-Whitworth and Humber cars. The former were built in Elswick Works, Newcastle on Tyne and two examples are seen in the foreground. The 17/25 hp chassis was advertised at £435 (with a free insurance policy!) while the limousine to the left was offered for £695 complete. In 1915 Armstrongs merged with Siddeley-Deasy of Coventry and no further cars were built in Newcastle. To the right, a 20 hp Humber tourer is visible.

An advert with a backdrop of Edinburgh Castle depicting a 38 hp Lanchester limousine which sold for the then not inconsiderable sum of £1075 (without extras as the publicity of the time pointed out). This Birmingham-built car appeared at the 1913 Motor Show which took place in Edinburgh's Waverley Market and its Scottish agent was the SMT Co. of Fountainbridge, Edinburgh and Reidvale Street, Glasgow. This was the same SMT which ran the buses, since the company was shrewd enough at an early stage to see a future both in public and private transport.

Well-known Glasgow motor agent Peter Holmes advertised the popular 'Bullnose' Morris Oxford for the initial appearance of this car at the 1914 Scottish Show. The Oxford was to be followed by the Cowley model introduced in 1915 which was also supplied by Holmes, the main Morris agent for Glasgow. Like the preceding 'Edwardian' shows, this one had been organised by the Scottish Motor Manufacturers and Traders Association (later to become the Scottish Motor Trade Association) which had been formed in 1903 and which still takes responsibility for the current Scottish Shows.

Scottish Show Stand № 38

Morris-Oxford
Light——Cars

London—Edinburgh
London to Schedule Time without adjustment, Full Marks

Dutch Reliability Trials (6 days)
First, no adjustment, Full Marks

Oxford Hill-Climbing Contest
First, Second, Third

10 h.p. De Luxe Model
190 Guineas

10 h.p. Standard Model
£180

10 h.p. Commercial Model
£175

10 h.p. De Luxe Model
Coupe

PETER HOLMES
AGENT
337-339 St. Vincent Street, GLASGOW

The MORRIS-OXFORD is the product of the combined knowledge and experience of several of the greatest Motoring Experts, and embodies in miniature the very best Large Car practice. It has been built to an Ideal—not a Price—with the object of making the Car the finest that brains can devise and skill produce. Furthermore, each individual part throughout the Chassis is constructed by firms that are acknowledged to be the Greatest Experts in their respective spheres   ::   ::

Scottis
MOTO
KELVIN HALL
GLASGOW

In 1925 Glasgow's Kelvin Hall was destroyed by fire and accordingly the Motor Show reverted to a venue in Edinburgh where it was held in the Industrial Hall in Annandale Street for 1925 and 1926. A new Kelvin Hall was built, however, and resumed as base for the Motor Show in 1927, remaining there until 1983 apart from a gap during wartime: in 1985 the Show was launched at its present location in the Scottish Exhibition & Conference Centre, Glasgow. This view at the corner of Argyle Street and Bunhouse Road shows the replacement Kelvin Hall under construction in July 1926 with YN 5794, a new London registered Armstrong- Siddeley 18 hp tourer posing outside.

Wee lads wanted to be just like their dads where motoring was concerned. Toy manufacturers had been well aware of this since the turn of the century and firms such as Lines Bros. in particular (better known as Tri-ang from 1931) produced a fine and remarkably realistic selection of different makes of pedal car based on the real thing. In 1929 Lumley's Emporium in Sauchiehall Street, Glasgow, introduced a children's motor show in their store to run in conjunction with that for the grown-ups at the Kelvin Hall. Today many of these early pedal cars are much sought after by collectors who occasionally pay more for the model than the cost of the original real car.

Robert Gibson & Sons of Cathcart was a subsidiary company of Harry Prosser & Sons of Glasgow. Their stand at the 1934 Scottish Motor Show at Kelvin Hall featured the American Studebaker from Indiana. On the left is the President Eight de luxe saloon the price of which was £435 plus £15 for a built-in wireless should that extra be desired. On the right was the Dictator Six Land Cruiser for £375 while centre was a 2 seater Studebaker roadster, believed to be the Commander Eight model.

Hillman and Humber cars at the stand of Anderson's of Newton Mearns at the 1936 Motor Show. While the show was held at the Kelvin Hall, not only cars but also components and commercial vehicles and buses were on display. This in many respects made for a more interesting exhibition but inevitably eventually brought complaints of insufficient space for cars whereas today's Motor Shows at Glasgow's SECC exclusively embrace private motoring. From the left the cars in this view are a Humber Eighteen saloon priced at £445; a Hillman Minx Magnificent de luxe, which offered fitted suitcases for an additional 3 guineas over the buying price of £175; a Humber Twelve saloon at £258 and a Hillman Sports Sixteen saloon. On display in the background is a Duple bodied Bedford coach in the 'Bluebird' livery adopted by Alexander of Falkirk.

Fifties, Sixties and beyond

Early 1950s in Henderson Street, Bridge of Allan, when gas lamps still provided illumination. CMS 560 is a 5 cwt. Fordson van of 1949, owned by a local window cleaner and passing Carmichael's Hotel and garage on the left while heading towards the camera is BGG 29 a 1938 Wolseley. It is followed by one of a large fleet of Leyland Titan double deckers purchased by Walter Alexander of Falkirk in the late 1940s and is passing through the village on the service from Dunblane to Cowie.

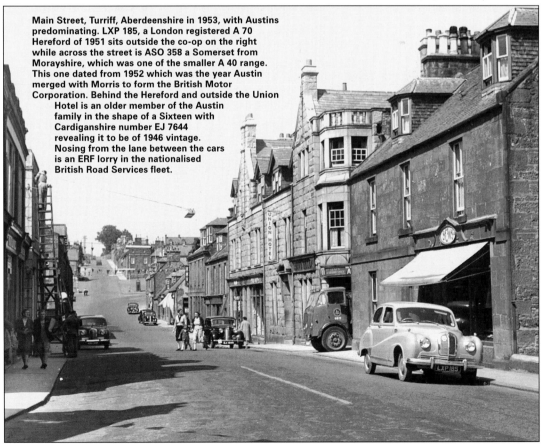

Main Street, Turriff, Aberdeenshire in 1953, with Austins predominating. LXP 185, a London registered A 70 Hereford of 1951 sits outside the co-op on the right while across the street is ASO 358 a Somerset from Morayshire, which was one of the smaller A 40 range. This one dated from 1952 which was the year Austin merged with Morris to form the British Motor Corporation. Behind the Hereford and outside the Union Hotel is an older member of the Austin family in the shape of a Sixteen with Cardiganshire number EJ 7644 revealing it to be of 1946 vintage. Nosing from the lane between the cars is an ERF lorry in the nationalised British Road Services fleet.

Staying in Aberdeenshire, this scene shows the main A96 Aberdeen to Inverness road through Inverurie around the same period. Immediately catching the eye is GSA 832, a locally registered Austin Atlantic of 1951 parked between Laing's Ford van and the Morris Commercial van. The line of parked cars has a splendid selection of family cars of the 'fifties, including Ford Prefects, Zephyrs, Riley, Vauxhall, Austin and Morris makes. The local bus beside the town hall was Easton's Duple bodied Bedford OB which ran to Pitcaple.

Main Street, Aberfoyle in 1954 looking towards the Bailie Nicol Jarvie hotel at the corner where the Trossachs road winds steeply up the hill from the village and the minor road ahead leads to Kinlochard and ultimately reaches Inversnaid on Loch Lomondside. In the foreground is HYS 511 which was a Singer SM 1500 of 1950, followed by an older Singer 10 and an Austin A 40, both with luggage on their roof racks suggesting holiday visitors to this attractive area.

The only sign of life in this mid 1950s view of Princes Street, Thurso is provided by the dog crossing from the Pentland Hotel where LUS 204 a 1953 Ford Prefect waits. Facing is EST 352 a 1951 Hillman Minx from Invernessshire while a Vauxhall Cresta disappears down the street past a parked Bedford van.

Crossgate in the county town of Cupar in Fife, looking towards the old Mercat Cross. Locally registered JFG 218 is a Standard Vanguard of 1950 which was that company's first post-war offering while across the street outside Woolworth's is HGD 743 a 1950 Morris Isis from Glasgow beside an older pre-war Austin Seven. Driving down from the junction with the A 91 Stirling to St Andrews road is an immediate post-war Austin Eight.

Queensferry Road in the north-west Edinburgh suburb of Blackhall is seldom seen so bereft of traffic today but in this scene from 1955 everything appears so much more leisurely and civilised although this wasn't necessarily appreciated by folks at the time. City-bound and passing David Jack's paint shop on the right is LSF 315, a 1954 Austin Somerset with a distant Jowett Javelin descending the hill behind.

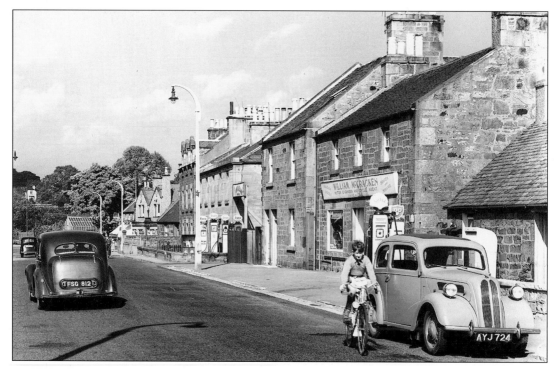

In the same area of Edinburgh, the adjoining suburb of Davidson's Mains is just a little closer to the River Forth, towards Cramond. In this view along the main street in June 1955 we see parked outside McCracken's Garage AYJ 724 which was a 1950 Ford Anglia from Dundee. The older car is locally registered FSG 812, a 1947 Humber Hawk which was typical of the large and solid family saloons still available at that time, with the traditional running boards and luggage boot.

A 1954 view of Union Street, Aberdeen, which has been carefully disguised by the photographer to appear more modern since he has masked out the tramway rails and overhead wires which were still in position until after the city withdrew the system in 1958. FRS 977, a local Rover P4 of 1954 drives towards us and parked outside the Queen's Cinema on the left is ECS 61, a 1952 Austin Atlantic from Ayrshire. On the right are a couple of Standard Vanguards and a Vauxhall Wyvern while all the double deck buses visible are Daimlers in the Corporation Transport fleet.

Football crowds throng Moss Street in Paisley on a mid 1950s Saturday afternoon. A Standard Vanguard is parked on the left as XS 7275 a 1951 Paisley registered Austin A 40 Devon drives past Glover's newsagency. Squeezing through the homegoing St Mirren supporters is GHS 994, a Leyland Titan double decker purchased in 1954 by McGill's Bus Service of Barrhead, a company which has only recently sold out after over three quarters of a century in the bus business to Arriva, major players in the transport field.

Bridge Street on Glasgow's southside in May 1958, where two very different types of Standard cars may be seen, bearing in mind that to a Glaswegian a car (or caur) meant a tramcar. The kind which did not run on rails were motors to them and so ESN 852 came into the latter category. It was a 1955 Standard Eight, while the Corporation Standard tramcar no. 231 dated back to the Edwardian era. Heading towards the city is MGA 983 which was a Vauxhall Velox of 1954 and visible behind the tram on the crossover is one of the Coronation type, so called as they were introduced at the time of the Coronation of King George VI in 1937.

A 1957 scene in King Street, Aberdeen when the tram tracks and electric overhead wires were still intact. Parked outside one of the many traditional granite-built terraced homes in the city is JKF 783 an early example of a Vauxhall Velox which bears a Liverpool index number from 1948, when this model was introduced. Behind it is KRS 392, an Aberdonian Ford Consul of 1957 while the passing bus which had travelled from Peterhead via Ellon was HMS 236 an AEC Reliance introduced to Alexander's 'Bluebird' fleet in 1956, which always carried Stirlingshire registrations because the company headquarters were in Falkirk.

Drumnadrochit, Invernessshire is the location in the early 1960s with interest provided by a late example of a Ford V8 Pilot which was registered BS 3507 in Orkney in 1950. The Bedford bus owned by Highland Omnibuses of Inverness is not quite what it seems since it started life in 1944 when it carried a wartime utility body with wooden slatted seats but in 1953 was rebodied as a coach by Burlingham of Blackpool which much modernised its appearance. When Highland sold AST 951 in 1964 it enjoyed a further lease of life in South Uist where it operated with MacDonald of Howmore.

Conon Bridge in the Easter Ross village of the same name in the late 1950s when it was still a temporary structure built over the original which had been damaged by heavy tanks which used it during wartime. Crossing the bridge which carried the old main A9 road between Beauly and Inverness is VGB 645 which was a Ford Prefect of 1958 being hotly pursued by a Highland Omnibuses Guy Arab on service from Dingwall to Inverness. Like so many other buses in this fleet it had an interesting pedigree having originally operated as a double decker with London Transport during World War 2. The SMT group, of which 'Highland' was a member, purchased a number of these vehicles in 1952, rebuilt them in their Marine Workshops at Portobello to single deck specification as seen and re-registered them, this one becoming JWS 124. Behind the bus at the end of the bridge on the left may be seen the garage premises where Frank Menzies built his various vehicles (see p. 40).

A Le Mans-like start from the traffic lights in Glasgow's Victorian city centre at the junction of Renfield and Gordon Street in 1966, when this was Forsyth's corner. Looks like a Ford Anglia in the lead, with a Zephyr on its left and Minis coming up on its right (the Mini celebrated its 40th birthday in 1999). Other cars visible among the tea-time sprinters are examples of

Riley, Morris Minor, Austin A55 and Hillman Imp, and also BMC FX4 taxicabs. The Corporation buses are mainly half-cab Leyland Titans of the late 1950s and the newer Leyland Atlanteans (badged as Albions!) which replaced the last of the city trams in the early 1960s.

Summer 1964 in East High Street, Forfar. In the immediate right foreground is a Morris Minor, while a split-windscreen van version owned by the post office stands a little way behind. Austin A30 FTS 445 of 1956 approaches while a brand new 1964 Austin Cambridge estate car heads the other way past Green Street. At the bus stop is Alexander (Northern) KWG 567, a 1958 AEC Reliance en route for Dundee.

Volume car production returned to Scotland in 1963 after a long absence. Linwood in Renfrewshire was chosen as the location for the Rootes Group plant where they built the Hillman Imp, their answer to the Mini. Also constructed here were the Hillman Hunter and from 1976 the Avenger on a site adjacent to where the Pressed Steel Co. had previously produced coupe bodies for Volvo. The giant Chrysler Corporation from the USA later acquired control until 1979 when they sold the troubled company to the French Peugeot-Citroen Group who revived the Talbot name at Linwood. The whole complex including Pressed Steel closed in May 1981 adding to Scotland's long list of failed motor manufacturers. Seen at an east coast fishing harbour, OHS 902F is a reminder of a 1968 example of the 875 cc rear-engined Imp which was discontinued after an unlucky 13 year life in 1976.

The Parabug to quote from its builder's publicity was 'the first all-action military style body kit to come on the British market'. This was in the early 1970s and could be purchased either in kit form or completely assembled from the manufacturers, North East Glassfibre Ltd., of Tullos, Aberdeen. The off-road vehicle utilised both chassis and engine from the Volkswagen Beetle and the illustration shows an early example on demonstration. Very few were constructed.

Other attempts at post-war car manufacture in Scotland included the Potts racing cars of the 1950s at Bellshill, Probe sports cars in the early 1970s at Irvine, the Haldane (which may be classed as a 'replicar' of the Austin Healey) between 1988 and 1994 at Blantyre then East Kilbride and the AC at Hillington. All of these were sporty examples and sadly ultimately doomed to extinction like so many of their predecessors. In the 1980s former aero engineer Bob Henderson revived the Argyll name for his turbo-charged high performance sports car and the first production model was launched by the Duke of Argyll in 1983. The stylish yet robust mid-engined 2.6 litre V6 G.T. as illustrated had many fittings built to aircraft, rather than automobile, specification and the long wheelbase of 9' 10" gave superb high speed stability. This second generation Argyll car is still available and can be built to individual customer requirements.

125

No parking problems with the Scamp! Built at Prestwick Airport by Scottish Aviation during the mid 1960s, this was a battery powered car whose name neatly united its Scottish parentage with the fact that it was an electric vehicle. Plans were made to market the car through Electricity Board showrooms but as with so many previous Scottish cars, things went wrong. The high cost of batteries with a suitably long life was one of the major problems and total production eventually numbered only around a dozen. One of these may be seen today in the Motoring Heritage Museum at the former Argyll Motor Works, Alexandria while another has been restored by the Royal Scottish Museum in Edinburgh. The first illustration shows one of the earliest models of 1965, with the cyclop's eye headlight, while the more conventional style of lighting design was applied to the later cars seen under construction at Prestwick in 1967.

As the new millennium breaks the only motor vehicles now produced in quantity in Scotland are the 'Green Machine' from Applied Sweepers in Falkirk and the Scot-Track from Nairn and although neither are motor cars they deserve mention. The former is a sweeper for use either in industrial premises or on the streets which since the late 1960s has in addition to home use been successfully exported to thirty countries world-wide. Meanwhile Scot-Track has built an all-terrain workhorse since 1988 in various forms of highway and off-road design at the Balmakeith Industrial Estate, Nairn. In addition to customers in Europe this company has also enjoyed world-wide export success to countries in the Middle-East, North America and Japan. The model illustrated is the HillCat 1700 which features a 46 hp turbo diesel engine and servo assisted hydrostatic transmission capable of transporting three personnel plus 750 kg of equipment over extreme terrain. Its simple yet rugged design makes it ideal for operations remote from technical support.

An addition to the list of Scottish motor manufacturers appeared in 1998. This was Rotor Motive Ltd. of Rutherglen whose proprietor Graham Millar had previously designed and constructed several small lightweight racing cars in the 1980s. Encouraged by their earlier success Rotor Motive are once again producing racing cars. Pictured is the prototype Ford-engined Rotor JT7 which has been favoured with complimentary press reports. It incorporates a tubular space-frame chassis with a mid-engine layout offering superior traction, road holding and handling. Given the success it deserves the Rotor will hopefully see the return of low-volume car production to Scotland.

This farewell photograph shows Strathpeffer Square and the Free Church spire from the Spa Pavilion with two small girls looking back from a typical large touring car of the late 1920s.

Reflecting on Scotland's first motoring century we must agree that it has been one of excitement and great development, much of which took place over the early years. What next century holds is anyone's guess but as standardisation increases apace there is little doubt that for sheer interest and variety of vehicles it is unlikely that any future period will compare with that which has gone.

Acknowledgements

My grateful thanks to the many motoring men and women who have helped over the years with relevant information and photographs including Tim Amyes, Ross Finlay, John Gillham, Jim Hunter, Peter Leask, Ian MacLean, Peter MacNab, the late George Oliver, Stan Prosser, Jim Savage, William Sleigh, Richard Stenlake, Bob Thomson, Jim Thomson, Andrew Webster, Bob Charnley (collection) and the Grampian Transport Museum. Front cover digital artwork by Ian Clydesdale, Scotart.com. I apologise to anyone I may have inadvertently overlooked.